Memoirs
of an
Eccentric Angel

Volume 1:

Fire & Ice

Judy Bohning

For information about this title or to order other books and/or electronic media, contact the publisher:

Atkins & Greenspan Publishing

TwoSistersWriting.com

18530 Mack Avenue, Suite 166

Grosse Pointe Farms, MI 48236

ISBN 978-1-956879-22-3 (Hardcover)

ISBN 978-1-956879-21-6 (Paperback)

ISBN 978-1-956879-23-0 (eBook)

Printed in the United States of America

All the stories in this work are true.

Cover Art: Judy Bohning

Cover and Graphic Design: Illumination Graphics

All photographs are part of the Bohning family's private collection.

Contents

I dedicate this book to

My late parents Dorothy and Wallace Bohning—
Who blessed me with the independence and strength that I have
needed throughout my life.

My dear friend Lori Cook Flatley—
Who always told me how courageous I was.
You, Lori, are the courageous one.

And—
To all the people who read this book and who are going through
a trauma. I hope you find the courage and strength you need to
move happily forward.

Acknowledgments

I want to thank Martin Sheen for putting the idea of this book in my head. I was writing a screenplay when, in one of our many phone conversations, he told me, "Judy, don't write a screenplay, write your memoirs."

I laughed and asked, "Who is going to read my memoirs? I'm nobody."

In the most stern, fatherly voice, he said, "Trust me, they'll read it."

For this, Martin, I am forever grateful.

I want to thank Catherine Greenspan for listening to a few of my stories and turning me on to her sister, Elizabeth Ann Atkins.

I want to thank my Book Coach Extraordinaire, Elizabeth Ann Atkins. Without your knowledge and guidance, I would never have seen my dream of a book come true after twenty-plus years.

I'm grateful for the graphic design expertise of Deborah Perdue of Illumination Graphics.

And thank you, Two Sisters Writing & Publishing, for bringing my book into the world.

Introduction

"Many of life's failures are people who did not realize how close they were to success when they gave up."

— Thomas Edison[1]

"History has demonstrated that the most notable winners usually encountered heartbreaking obstacles before they triumphed. They won because they refused to become discouraged by their defeats."

— B.C. Forbes[2]

FOR THE LAST TWENTY-SOME YEARS, I HAVE HAD these two quotes taped to my bathroom mirror and at my computer. I have always looked at them as very powerful statements. I truly believe they have helped me to continue on. I can say that these quotes were what pushed me to write this book.

I also didn't want to give up five minutes before the miracle. I have been through a lot, and these experiences were not only my obstacles, but my triumphs as well. I refused to quit, no matter how discouraged I became.

Quitting is not an option.

I have always been an optimist and tried to look at the glass as half full. However, I am the first to admit that in times of trauma and grief, it is hard to keep an upbeat attitude about life. You might even find yourself asking God why this situation has happened to you. I heard once that God only gives you as much as He knows you can handle.

I have yet to decide if God is a man or a woman, or both. This is a question I look forward to learning the answer to. I believe that once we die, we will find out the answer to questions we have here on earth.

For example, when my home burned down, they investigated for four days and never came up with a reason the fire started. I would love to be able to ask God that question and find out what really happened to my home.

I have not written about the house fire in this book because, to me, I didn't want it to be a "Debbie Downer" type of book. There are enough tragedies in this first book that I felt the house fire added in was a little too much. So, you will hear about the house fire most likely in my next volume of the series when it comes out.

I have reflected on my life experiences and wonder at times, "How did I make it out of situations basically unscathed, and for what reason? What is it that I am supposed to do in my life?" I figure that God didn't give me all of these experiences not to share them with you, and that's the reason for the book. When I tell people of my close calls, they just look at me like, "How are you still here?"

My only answer to that is, "My Guardian Angel Bob."

Bob has been a very busy guardian; I'm glad he's watching over me. I am thankful for all the angels that we on earth are blessed with.

I once read somewhere that if, right before you go to sleep, you ask your guardian angel their name, they will answer you within about ten days' time. I remember asking my angel what his or her name was for about four nights in a row. On the fifth morning, I was in that half-asleep/half-awake mode when, in the back right side of my brain, I heard the name Bob. I shot right up in bed and questioned,

"Bob? Really? Your name is Bob?"

For the next week, I went to bed at night asking if that was really his name. He has never answered. So, my guardian angel's name is Bob.

I believe we all have guardian angels. For instance, I sometimes wonder if my daughter's guardian angel is my father. If he were alive, she would have been the cream in his coffee, the frosting on his cake. She would have stolen my spot as Daddy's Little Girl. I believe he is the one watching over and protecting her now.

I named this book *Memoirs of an Eccentric Angel* because I've always considered myself eccentric; the definition of eccentric is deviating from the norm, and I've never thought of myself as normal.

I'm sharing these stories with you in the hopes that they will inspire you to stay strong when circumstances seem impossible, when you're hurting, when you're wondering, "Why me?"

Please enjoy the read and apply the lessons and wisdom to your life, so that you can truly make every day as happy as possible.

Smiles,

Judy Bohning

My Worst Three Months

IT WASN'T YOUR ORDINARY FRIDAY MORNING. I WAS LYING in bed, fast asleep, when the alarm clock went off, scaring the bajeezus out of me. I quickly flung my hand onto the top of the alarm, shutting it off. Rolling over, thinking, Do I *really have to get up this early? For God's sake, the sun isn't even up yet.* Just the tiniest slivers of light were coming from what will soon be the morning sun.

"Yes, you have to get up now if you want to go out tonight and play some Blackjack before you fly home tomorrow," said the devil on my left shoulder.

"But get your work done first," chimed the angel on my right.

I was working for a costume house in Los Angeles that was finishing the overflow of costumes for the new Bob Mackie show, which was opening that weekend at the MGM Grand Hotel in Las Vegas.

I reluctantly swung my legs over the edge of the bed, sat there for a few short minutes, turning on the bedside table lamp so I could see. I hadn't picked out my clothes for the day the night before, so I started burrowing through my suitcase for a top to wear. My best jeans were already lying on the bed. I put my black and white, diagonally-striped, long-sleeved, silk blouse on top of the jeans, a pair of black lace panties, with matching bra, of course, next to them, and striped socks to match.

At 5'9" and about 125 or 130 pounds, I loved to wear my good designer jeans with silk blouses and high heels.

I took off my panties from the night before and started to head to the bathroom. I heard a lot of commotion out in the hall. I couldn't quite make out what they were saying. I just chalked it up to it being an early Friday morning, about a quarter to five, and that they had been up all night partying and were a little loud heading back to their rooms. I paid no attention to them, walked across the room to the bathroom.

As I shut the door, I made sure to lock it. Any woman who grew up in the *Psycho* film era will understand what I am saying. Alfred Hitchcock was the best at scaring the daylights out of people. I could not get the shower scene in that movie out of my head, the blood, the music, and the suspense.

Nope, I can't be in a hotel bathroom without the door locked, I thought.

I turned on the shower to let it heat up, brushed out my hair, and checked the shower water. Ah, perfect, I climbed in, enjoying the hot water running down the back of my neck and back. I bent my head so that the water was spraying directly on my hair, getting it all wet to add the shampoo. While lathering it up, I rehearsed how I would approach Bob Mackie (he was Cher's costume designer) when he would come in today to check on the progress for the opening the next night. I wanted to hit him up for a job.

Hello, Mr. Mackie, my name is… No, no. *Excuse me, Mr. Mackie…* No, *don't start with that.* I was on automatic pilot as I washed my hair and body. All I could think about was, *What is the most professional way to handle the introduction to* Mr. Mackie? I must have been in the shower a good thirty minutes. It just felt so good. I reached out for the towel. I always dry off in the shower; it's too cold on the other side of the shower curtain. After I dried off, I stepped out of the shower, bent over and wrapped my hair in my towel. I then continued to dry my hair—which was long and blond at the time—curled it, and put on my makeup. This all took about an hour. I was slow.

Not that the joint I was smoking was slowing me down any. I found that smoking a joint in the morning while getting ready for my day was the best way to truly wake up. It acted as my cup of coffee, as I do not drink any. Never could acquire a taste for coffee. I love the smell and I can make a great cup; I just don't care for the bitterness of it. Not even coffee candy. I do admit I will eat coffee ice cream, if that's all that is offered, but it would never be a desired flavor.

With my makeup on, I flipped my hair upside down and whipped it back, fluffed up the curls a bit, and I was ready to get dressed. Stark-ass naked as I opened the door to my room, I stood there for a brief second, taking in the fact that my room was pitch black. Thinking out loud: "Now, I know I'm not that high! It was starting to get light out when I went into the bathroom, and I've been in there a good hour and a half. What is going on?"

I remembered Mom telling me a story about when she was at O'Hare Airport in Chicago. She told me how everything went black;

you couldn't see a thing. Turns out it was a very bad thunderstorm rolling through. *Maybe that's what is going on?*

I made my way over to the other side of the bed near the window to find the stack of clothes I had laid out with my jeans earlier.

Right about that time, I suddenly heard voices in the hall:

"Fire, fire, we've got to get out!"

At that very moment, I could smell the smoke. It was a smell I will never forget. The smell of burning plastics, fabrics, chemicals from the paint, and God knows whatever else. It was unlike anything I had ever smelled before, nor do I care to again. Little did I know.

"FUCK!!!" I exclaimed. "FIRE!!! What the hell do I do now? Getting dressed would be a good start."

I tried to look out my window. The MGM building was built in the shape of a square, and my room was on the inside of the building with the theater down on ground level. This made the middle section above the theater like a chimney, with all the smoke barreling upward toward the sky. It was as if someone had painted my window black, it was so dark.

I started feeling around on the bed for the stack of clothing. I found it toward the middle of the bed. I had to feel around for the items as I need them and dressed in the dark. It was not like I hadn't dressed in the dark before, but this was a different dark. You couldn't see your hand in front of your face. No backlight from under the hallway door, no light from the window, nothing. It was total darkness, with a very eerie quiet that went along with it for a brief moment. It was like someone turned off the audio and I could only see and smell. Then the voices from the hall started up again.

Once I was dressed, I made my way over to the door, opened it, and the smoke was at knee level. I ran into a gal and her mother, who said, "We came down the fire stairs from the sixteenth floor, but when we got to the twelfth floor, the fire doors were locked. So, we came back up to this floor. What do we do from here?"

She was asking as if I had done this before and knew what to do.

I replied, "My room is totally black. Let's knock on the door across the way."

Sure enough, someone answered the door. The gentleman let us in their room as his wife was in hysterics. She just knew we were all going to die!

I have to admit, the thought of never seeing anyone I ever knew or loved again was a distinct possibility at the present moment. Inside, I was scared shitless, but something just clicked and switched me into another mode. Survival mode!

I remained very calm, even with a screaming, distraught Canadian woman shrieking in the background. She smelled like she had been drinking all night. The coffee table in front of the couch showed evidence of such. There was a bottle of bourbon with just a drop left in it, and two used tumbler glasses on the table as well.

I first went to the bathroom to soak a couple of bath towels in water to put at the bottom of the door to the hallway in an attempt to keep some of the smoke from entering our room.

I tried to get any kind of information I could. First, I turned on the television. Nothing. I then tried the radio. Nothing. The telephone only gave me a busy signal. We were basically on our own.

I knew that you were not supposed to open anything for fear of a backdraft, but there was no fire, just smoke, and lots of it. I went over to the window, pressing my ear to the glass. They had firemen on the ground with blow horns giving instructions. I just couldn't make out what they were saying. I went ahead and opened the window, just about an inch, to hear what was being said.

When I had put my ear to the window, I was looking in the direction of the front of the building. It was totally engulfed with flames and thick, black smoke. It was one of the most frightening, intimidating, and threatening things I have ever seen. To think that I was inside this burning building was like an out-of-body experience where I was watching the evening news, not that I could possibly be a part of this horrific happening.

I had a hard time concentrating on what was being said because the noises all around me were more of a distraction than I had ever experienced. People were throwing furniture out of the windows above us. It was a 26-story high-rise building built in 1972, opening in December of 1973, of which we were right in the middle. No using the elevators, nor the stairs, and no fire ladders were coming to our rescue. Do you know that in 1980, fire ladders, I believe, only went as high as the ninth floor? We were on the thirteenth floor, just a few floors too high.

The noises from the helicopters were very loud. It seemed as if one was flying over continuously, but in reality, it was one right after the other. I couldn't tell you how many copters they had in the sky, but it was a good half dozen. They just kept coming and coming. The sounds of furniture flying out of windows started up again. People were screaming for help. It was a very horrific event that felt extremely dire. I knew my options were very limited.

I had brought my purse with me, and I dug into it to retrieve my Red Swiss Army Knife that I always carried with me. In my mind at this point, I figured I had two options: I could be a pancake or a marshmallow. I chose pancake. If the fire started to come through the door, I was going out the window on my rope.

I went over to the bed that was made, threw back the blanket down to the sheets. I took one of the top flat sheets and started to tear apart about ten-inch wide strips. If nothing else, I was going to make a rope out of them by knotting the sections together, and do my darnedest to try and climb down as far as possible until someone could get a fire ladder to me. I figured that should be strong enough to hold me. No, the idea of burning alive just didn't thrill me any. At least this way I was in control, and if it was my time, it would be my way.

Once the commotion quieted a bit, I could barely make out what they were saying to us: "Just sit tight for now. Firemen will be around to each and every room to assist in your safe departure from the building. Please do not try to leave your room on your own. Be patient; we have many people to help out of this and we will be around to get you. Just please remain in your rooms and wait for the firemen. Thank you."

They specifically said, "The fire is out and there are no major concerns. Just sit and wait for the firemen."

A couple of hours into this horrific ordeal, I pulled the gal into the bathroom and said, "Since the fire is out, I'm going to go across to my room and get my suitcase. If I'm not back in five minutes, come get me."

She was somewhat concerned. "Don't go," she said, "you really shouldn't leave the room. You heard what the fireman said."

I explained, "I have all of my good silk blouses and Italian leather heels in my bag. I will not leave without them. Or the ounce of pot that just happens to be there, too." I *was going to be there a while, what can I say*? I thought.

"Don't worry," I said. "I'll be back before the five minutes is up. I'll be fine. They said the fire was out, so there is nothing to worry about. I'll be right back."

I went into the bathroom to get a wet washcloth to cover my face. I opened the door and the smoke in the hallway was a little clearer. It was now about chest high. I went across the hall to my room and found that my door was ajar. I thought that was a little odd, but I had left in a hurry. The smoke had cleared a bit, at least enough to see what was going on. I grabbed my belongings, including the marijuana.

I got everything into my suitcase and looked out the window saying, "The police lied to us, the theater is still on fire." I quickly grabbed my bag and went back across the hall to the Canadian couple's room.

I was feeling completely lied to and betrayed. I *understand that there are a lot of people here, but do they have to lie to us*? Yes, it could cause undo panic, but they just lied!

Once I was back in the room, I pulled Diane into the bathroom again to tell her, "Don't say anything, except to your mother, but the theater is still on fire. They have totally lied to us. I don't want this lady freaking out on us anymore. She's a little over the top. Especially since I believe we will all make it out of this. It just may take some time."

The sounds of the helicopters seemed to go on forever. I don't recall how many hours people were still throwing furniture out of the windows. They just needed to be able to breathe.

We were all fidgety. Some of us would sit down for a bit while the others paced the room. We would switch back and forth, while not much was being said. It was rather quiet, but given the circumstances, I suppose no one felt like talking too much. We were all very encompassed in our own thoughts.

What would we do when we got out of this mess? Who were we thinking about, and would we see them again? Whom would we call first?

We sat around for about four hours, and then there was a knock at our door. I got up to answer it, and there stood a tall fireman with full gear on, coming into our room. He explained what was going on.

"Most of the fire is towards the front of the building," he said. "So, what we're going to do is, I want everyone to get a wet washcloth. I'm going to be leading you down to the next floor. From there, we're going to walk to the back of the building to the stairs at that end. Now, as we're walking, do not touch the walls. They are very hot. Once we get to the stairs, you will be on your own to walk all the way down to the ground floor. Are there any questions?"

"May I take my suitcase with me?" I asked.

No one said a word. Since I was being ignored, I just went ahead and started carrying my suitcase with me.

"Okay, let's go," the fire fighter said. "My partner will be in front leading us, and I'll follow up the rear. You are all safe."

The two firemen led us out of the room and down the hall to the stairs. The fireman bringing up the rear took my suitcase from me, saying, "Let me get this."

We went down one flight of stairs to the twelfth floor. As we were walking along the twelfth floor hallway, I totally understand how the Twin Towers collapsed. They melted. The fireman did not need to tell us not to touch the walls; it was like we were walking through an oven at 500 degrees. You could feel the heat radiating off them. It felt as if we were walking through Hell, and in a way, I guess we were. The heat was so intense, it was almost unbearable, but with our adrenaline pumping to the max, it really wasn't the first thing on our minds. The most important item to attend to was getting out of this building in one piece.

The fireman was kind enough to carry my suitcase down the stairs, and all the way to the back of the building. Then he said, "This is as far as I can help you with this. I need to go back for others."

I said, "Thank you so very much for carrying my suitcase all the way down the hall. I certainly appreciate it. I also totally understand. Go, save more people, you're good at it!"

I started walking down the long stairwell. It wouldn't have been too bad if I hadn't been toting my large suitcase with me. The ladies reading this should understand, you don't leave silk clothing and Italian heels behind. Call me shallow, but you just don't. It seemed to take me forever to make my way down the stairs. Everyone was passing me as I stopped to take short breaks, but I didn't care. I could care less how long it took me to get to the ground floor. Nothing of mine was being left behind. I worked too hard and too long to acquire the things I had. It wasn't much, but it was mine and I bought them, not some man trying to get into my pants.

I made it! I made it to the ground and out the door of that horrible experience. I took a couple steps on the sidewalk and then just stopped, frozen in shock. A young, good-looking gentleman was standing there and I said, "Excuse me, but could I have a hug, please!"

I needed that hug to know that I was alive and I had made it out fairly unscathed.

The young man was happy to oblige by saying, "My goodness, were you in the building? How horrible that must have been. I'm more than happy to give you a hug."

He gave me one very long hug. Good enough to know I was still alive.

"Thank you so very much," I said. "You have no idea how much I needed that. Just knowing that I made it out alive and I'm here and in one piece. Thank you again, thank you!"

I was overjoyed with feeling alive. I don't think I have ever experienced anything as close to death before. Except for maybe the time that I was hit by a train. That incident had its own terror attached to it. But that's a tale for another time.

After I thanked him and his friends, I started walking. I didn't know where I was going. I guess I was looking for someone who could tell me what was next in this little adventure of mine. All of a sudden, I ran into Diane and her mother, also wondering what was next.

Marge said, "The man at the corner said we were all to gather at the casino across the street. I believe it was the Barclay, not too sure."

Off we went in the direction of the casino, just to be continually turned back as all the fire equipment was in the roadway. They told us we could walk around the block to get there. Now, if you're old enough to remember Vegas in the early 1980s, have you ever tried walking around a block in Las Vegas? They are huge and takes forever. I wasn't about to go that route unless absolutely necessary. I spotted a parking lot across the street that looked to be the back parking for the Barclay Casino.

I said, "Look, we can walk down a bit and cut through the parking lot, much easier!"

We headed to the entry of the parking lot, walking towards the Barclay. Halfway into the lot, we encountered a slight obstacle—a six-foot-high cinderblock wall dividing the two parking lots. The three of us, plus two others that followed us out of curiosity, stood there looking at the wall. I was young and fairly athletic.

I sized up the wall and said, "I figure if I get a good enough running start, I could scale it fairly easy. Then I could sit up on top of the wall to help everyone else over. Diane, would you go after me so that you're on the other side already when your mother goes over next?"

We all agreed on that plan of action. I backed up about three or four car lengths, got in the set position, and off I went for the wall. As I got closer to it, I was ready to throw my right leg up to scale the darn thing, when all of a sudden I realized, *Fuck, I grabbed the wrong pair of jeans! These are my tight ones. There's no getting over this wall that way.*

I looked around and a couple of cars down were cement posts between the cars and the wall. I thought about it for a moment and figured,

Okay, if I can't get a running start, then maybe I can just climb up to the top.

So I asked, "Here, Diane, would you hold this for me please?"

I gave her my purse and stood on the bumper of a car to climb on top of this post.

"This is an interesting undertaking to try in cowboy boots," I said.

But from there, I was able to climb up to the top of the wall. I sat up there, straddling the wall so it would be easier to help the others over. Diane went over next. She just followed my lead. Bumper, post, I gave her a hand, and she made it to the wall. Then,

I helped lower her down gently to the ground on the other side.

There was a newly married couple with us. The gentleman helped Marge with each obstacle, and once I had her on the wall, her daughter helped from the other side to get her down. Next, the bride went over, and lastly, the husband, but not before handing my suitcase to me so I could pass it over to Diane on the other side. I then swung my other leg over the wall, turned around, holding onto the top of the wall, and lowered myself as far as I could, then just dropped the last couple of feet. Success! We all made it over and off to the lobby to check in.

A policeman had told us that we were all to check into the Barclay so they could get an accurate account of who made it out and from which rooms. The lines were quite long at the reception desk. We sat down in one of the lines as this was going to take a while.

I turned to Diane and said, "I'm going to see if I can find the payphones. I need to make a couple of calls. I'll be back in a bit."

"Okay, we'll be here," Diane responded.

I found the phones. They were actually rather close by. Of course, the lines were as long as the front desk lines. I went back to Diane and her mother and said, "I found the payphones, but the lines are just as long as here. Since this is going to take a while, Diane would you come let me know when it's close to our turn, please? I just have to get ahold of my mother. She's probably worried sick."

Diane responded, "No, I'll come get you when we're looking like we're close. You take care of your phone call. I agree, your mother must be going crazy not hearing from you."

"Thanks! I certainly appreciate it." And off I went to get in yet another line. The lines were forever long. Of course it was much too soon for cell phones. Ah, the good old days. Sometimes I wonder if we were better off then. I know as a child I felt very safe playing outside until dark.

They must have called in every cocktail waitress that worked for Barclay's. Everywhere you turned, there was a waitress with a tray of full drinks. It was just the generic bar booze. Guess they wanted to soothe the very raw nerves of all the MGM guests that were wandering around in all stages of dress.

As one was about to pass by me, I stopped her and said, "May I have two please? Rum and Coke if you have them."

"Yes, here you go," she said. "Help yourself at any time. Thank you." She turned and walked off. Now that I was prepared, I started to observe the different people around, not just me, but the casino in general.

I saw one woman in her chenille bathrobe, leopard print, of course, black pajama pants hanging below the hem of the robe, with the biggest, furriest leopard print slippers I have ever seen. Her hair was still wrapped up in her night scarf, glasses and a drink in her hand. Seeming as if she had absolutely no idea where to go, just a blank stare on her face.

There was a very elegant couple who must have been up all night. He had gorgeous silver hair and was in his black velvet tuxedo, and she with her curled, flowing red hair, was in a very form-fitting gown—olive green sequins, sleeveless, with a flare just below her buttocks, and only a shawl around her shoulders. She was carrying her high heels by this time, and frankly, I don't blame her, I would have, too.

It didn't seem that much later, but I found myself drink-less. I had downed both of those Rum and Cokes in a matter of minutes.

Another cocktail waitress was passing by.

"Do you have any Rum and Coke?" I asked.

"Certainly, here you go."

"May I have another? My nerves are a bit shot."

She replied, "You may have as many as you like. Were you in the fire?"

"Yes, I was on the fourteenth floor," I answered. "Really the thirteenth, you know how they never have a thirteenth floor in hotels. I was stuck up there for six hours. It was truly frightening."

"Well, you take care of yourself, dear." Off she went with her tray of drinks.

I didn't want to monopolize the phone, as there were only eight in the bank of phones. I was thinking of everyone I needed to call. Of course, Mom was first. I didn't want her to worry any more than necessary. I also needed to call Janet, my boss, to let her know what was happening here. Mainly that I was okay. I finally got my turn at a phone and immediately called my mother's home number. All I got was a busy signal. I tried several times and got the same signal.

Next, I tried calling my boss. I got through to her. She was watching it all unfold on her little fourteen-inch portable television.

"Are you alright?" Janet asked with a bit of a scare in her voice.

"Yes, I'm okay. It's been one hell of a morning, though. What do I do now?"

"Take my airplane ticket I gave you and use it to fly home tomorrow morning."

"That's fine, but what do I do tonight?" I asked.

"Just find a place to stay and fly back tomorrow," Janet said. "Let me know when you get back so I know you're safe and sound. Gotta run. Take care." Next thing I heard was a dial tone.

"That didn't go exactly as I had hoped," I said out loud.

Let's try Mom again, I thought. The line was still busy. I thought about calling my aunt, just to get a message to Mom. I dialed her number, and surprisingly, it rang.

"Hello," Hat said. That's short for Harriet.

"Hi, Hat. I'm okay, but could you please call Mom and let her know? I've been trying to get through to her for over a half hour, and I just get a busy signal. I made it out of the building okay, but it was scary as hell."

"Judy, what are you talking about?" she asked.

"The MGM Grand fire!!! Aren't you watching the news? I'm going to hang up now and try Mom again. You take care. Bye"

Once again, I called Mom's number, and success, I got through. I had been calm and composed throughout this entire ordeal, but as soon as I heard my mother's voice, I totally fell apart. I started crying, and all I could get out was, "I'm okay!!! I made it out all right, Mom. I'm okay," I said with tears flowing down my cheeks.

"What are you talking about?"

"You're okay? What's going on?"

"Geez, doesn't anyone up there watch the news? The MGM Grand Hotel is on fire!!!"

"Well, I know that, dear, I'm watching it on TV. But you're back home now, so why so upset about the fire?"

"Mom, I'm still here!!! I just got out of the building."

"I thought you went home to LA on Wednesday?" she asked.

"No, we left LA Wednesday to drive over to Vegas," I said. "I've been here since then. But I'm okay. I was stuck on the thirteenth floor for six hours, but I'm on the ground and I'm flying home tomorrow. So don't worry about me."

At this point, I had composed myself somewhat, but just couldn't stop crying. Then Mom started crying, and we couldn't make out a word either of us were saying.

"Look, Mom. I gotta go. I still have to check into the Barclay Casino so they know I made it out okay. Give Dad my love. I love you, too. I'll call you when I get home from here. Bye."

I had a couple more phone calls to make but was very nervous about the one to Michael, so I shelved it for the time being. Others were waiting to use the phones, so I went back to where I left Diane and Marge to see what was happening there.

I saw Diane and said, "Well, I finally got through to both my boss and my mother. She thought I was already home and wasn't worried a bit."

"That's good that she didn't realize you were here," Diane said. "I could just imagine what would be going through a mother's mind if she saw this on the news and knew her child was there. Horrifying!"

The line had at least moved halfway closer to the front desk. It seemed like forever, but we finally made it up to the counter where we could check in.

One at a time, we gave them the basic information: name, room number, how many people in the room, as well as our contact information. When we were all done, we walked a bit together and I asked, "What are you two going to do now?"

"We're going to try and find a room to stay in this evening," Diane said. "How about you?"

"I still need to make a couple of phone calls, then I'll be looking for a room, too, I guess. It was very nice meeting you, sorry it was under such stressful conditions. Do take care and travel safe," I said as they turned to walk off.

As they were leaving, Diane said, "Good luck to you, Judy. Thank you for all the help. We certainly appreciate it. It was really nice meeting you, just too bad it was under such terrible circumstances."

"Thank you as well," I replied. "You and your mother helped me through an ordeal that I'm glad I wasn't totally alone for. Good luck finding a place. It was wonderful meeting you, as well. Take care. Bye." I grabbed my suitcase and headed back to the bank of payphones. I had to admit, I was a bit on the frightened side, as I still had to make that call to Michael. I made my way to the phone line once again.

Another cocktail waitress was passing by and I asked, "Excuse me, may I have a couple Rum and Cokes, please?"

I took the two drinks from her and started to down one of them. I figured in the timeframe of about three hours, I had about nine or ten Rum and Cokes. My adrenaline was pumping so much that the alcohol had no effect. I was totally sober. I was really afraid of Michael, but knew I had to call him.

I tell myself, *Michael will be livid if I take this into my own hands and change the plans on him. But let's be honest, Judy, and somewhat sensible, too. You're very distraught and hysterical right now. This is the perfect time and condition to call the insurance man.* I have a hard time making pretty much any important, life-changing choices when I need to. But I did it. Since I could not get ahold of Michael, I made an executive decision. I got out my address book to look up Harry's number.

I downed the second drink to boost my courage. I thought about my phone call to Mom and how upset we were. I closed my eyes to get a better vision of Mom and me, both upset, to work myself back up to the hysterical point. That's when I dialed Harry's number and he answered.

"Harry," I said, sobbing, "it's Judy Bohning. I'm in the MGM fire and my ring is gone! I had to leave my room because of smoke, and when I went back, the door was ajar and my jewelry, including the diamond ring that was on the dresser, was gone." More sobbing and crying.

"Judy, calm down," Harry said. "I'm watching it on TV now. It will all be okay. You did the right thing and had it insured, so everything will be okay. Are you all right? Were you hurt at all?"

"I'm okay. Just really shaken up by all that's happened. I honestly don't know what end is up right now."

"Look, it will all be okay," Harry said calmly. "Get yourself back to town and give me a call when you're able to come into the office. We'll take care of everything we need to then. In the meantime, I'll at least get your claim started. So, take a deep breath and calm down. You are in good hands. You take care, now. It will all be all right. Travel safe. Goodbye."

Thinking, *Well, that went rather well.* I was wiping tears from my eyes and taking deep breaths, feeling much more calm and in control. Not that I ever really felt out of control, except for when I was thirteen stories in the air.

I had no idea what I was going to do, or where I was going to go next. I found myself a nice pillar that was somewhat private, out of the way of the hustling and bustling all around me. I set my suitcase down, then myself, on the floor next to it, wondering what was next. I was just staring off into the distance with a blank look on my face, thinking, *What a mess I've gotten myself into!*

FLASHBACK SIX MONTHS: It was the fifth of June, an ashy day early this morning in Southern Oregon. I wanted to say the air was crisp and clean, but sadly just a few weeks earlier, Mount St. Helens had erupted. Now, the air was almost choking with ash in each breath you would take. There was ash on my car every morning; it was a mess I had never experienced before. The ground and cars looked like there was a very light dusting of snow, when in actuality it was ash blowing south from Mount St. Helens.

I had just graduated from Design School and decided to drive home to spend a week with Tom, my future husband. At this point, we just spent time with one another when we could, but still saw others because of the distance, I guessed. I was living in LA, and Tom in Oregon, which didn't make it easy to have a relationship. He hated Los Angeles and made it very clear when I moved there that he would not be down to visit.

Tom was my first love. I met him the first week at college in Ashland at Southern Oregon College, as it was known by at the time. By this time, I had convinced myself that he was the first man I ever slept with who took my virginity.

However, that was not the case. I tried very hard at the time to convince myself that the rape didn't count because I had not given consent. It was a horrible weekend with my abduction, drugs, and rape that I cared to pretend didn't exist. I don't care to go into it at this point, but you will read all about it in the future. Let's stick to one "flashback" at a time.

Tom and I had just returned to the rustic little one-room cabin he was calling home these days. He worked as a bartender down the road a bit, and for now this was home. We had just eaten breakfast and had wanted to take the boat out on the Rogue River, but the ash in the air made that impossible. So, with a good meal in our stomachs, we decided to pull out the drugs—a little cocaine and some really good smoke I had brought up from LA with me. Tom had the cocaine because, little to my surprise, he was selling it on the side.

About thirty minutes into snorting and smoking, Tom said out of the blue, "You just got out of school and must owe a little money or be in need of some. Would that be correct?"

"I do owe about $2,500 for what I spent to make my costumes for graduation. A little extra cash wouldn't hurt, that's for sure."

"If you're interested, I have a proposition for you." He waited for me to say something.

"What's the proposition?" I asked.

"My cousin, Michael, has this little insurance scheme that he has done a few times, and it seems to work rather nicely," Tom replied.

"Insurance scheme? Are you talking insurance fraud?"

"Yes, you could call it that."

I came back with, "I don't know about that. I'm not the most honest person on the face of the earth, but I have never done anything like that before."

"Are you at least interested in listening to how it all works?" Tom asked.

"I suppose," I responded. "So, what happens? Are the police involved at some point? I can't do anything that involves the police. Sorry, but that's just a little too sketchy for me."

"The only time the police are involved is when you report a diamond ring stolen from you," he said. "They just take the report. You have proof of the ring because you had it appraised. However, the ring you will be wearing around your friends to let it be known that you have this ring will be a fake. Make up some sort of story as to how you got it. Maybe it was a gift from a rich sugar daddy; I don't know, you can think of something."

He continued, "Michael will provide a diamond ring for you to take and get appraised. Once you have the appraisal, then you take out an insurance policy on the ring. You will give the diamond ring Michael gives you back to him, and you go out and get a CZ that you wear around for your friends to see, so people know you have a nice ring. After four to six months, then we will arrange a little break-in at your apartment, and the ring is stolen. This is where I come in. I'm the one that breaks into your apartment. Once that happens, then you file a police report for the stolen diamond ring."

I sat there quietly for a few minutes, then said, "I really don't know. This all sounds a little too sketchy for me. And the last thing I want to do is have to talk to the police about it. I'll have to lie right to their faces, and honestly, I don't know if I can do that part."

Tom replied, "That's the easy part. By that time, it's all over and you just need the police report to turn into the insurance company to be paid. It's not that difficult."

"It may not be that difficult for you, but I've never lied to a policeman before. I'm just not too sure about this."

"Will you at least think about it?" Tom asked.

"I'll think about it, but don't hold your breath," I replied.

Two weeks later, I was home in my apartment in LA going through a pile of bills and thinking about Tom's proposition. I was thinking of the pro's and con's of this whole diamond situation.

I could really use the money. Tom did point out it's not like we're stealing from one person. It's a big company that does this for a living, and they are making a pretty penny from it. It just doesn't feel right to me, though. Maybe

I'll just let Tom introduce me to Michael, and I can go from there. Little did I know, just where it would go and what all it was going to involve. I knew it was wrong, but I picked up the phone to call Tom.

"Hello, Tom. I've been thinking about what you had offered while I was up in Oregon. I'm willing to meet Michael, but this is not a 'Yes, I'll do it.'"

"Great. I'll give Michael a call tonight and we can arrange a time for me to come down there to introduce the two of you."

"Alright, I've got a lot to do, so I'm going to let you go now. I'll talk to you later." I hung up.

A week later, to my surprise, Tom was in Los Angeles, and called me: "Hi, I'm here in Southern Cal, out at Michael and Marla's house in Calabasas. When can you get together for a little meet and greet?"

"Well, I guess tomorrow is good. I suppose the sooner the better for you, so you can get the heck out of here? How about the two of you coming by my place about two, tomorrow afternoon?"

Tom checked the time with Michael and said, "Two o'clock it is, then. You have a good night."

"I will. You do the same. Goodbye." I hung up the phone, feeling somewhat guilty and I hadn't even done anything yet. Who knew if I would even go through with this?

The next day arrived and I found myself very apprehensive about this afternoon's meeting. It sounded somewhat easy. It would be nice to be out of debt.

I guess I'll see how it goes and make up my mind from there.

Two o'clock rolled around and I found myself pacing the apartment from my bedroom to the kitchen, through the living room and back to my bathroom in my room. I was so nervous, I couldn't sit still. I kept looking at my watch, which didn't seem to be moving because I was looking at it every three seconds.

Suddenly, there was a knock at the front door. I took one last look at myself in the mirror and headed for the door. I opened it, and there stood Tom with a slightly taller man, about 6'2". He looked a little like Peter Fonda—tall, thin, and somewhat handsome. However, he had a slight shady look to him, kind of like Eddie Haskell from *Leave it to Beaver*. You wanted to trust him, but something in your gut said, "Run!"

I said to both of them, "Come in and make yourselves comfortable. Can I get you anything to drink?"

Michael spoke up, "Water will be just fine. Thank you."

Tom agreed, "Water sounds good."

I went to the kitchen to get some waters for all of us. I was not gone but two minutes, and when I returned to the living room, it hadn't taken the boys long at all to pull out a mirror and start fixing lines. I just looked at them and said, "I guess I did say to make yourselves comfortable. Would you like some smoke to go along with the blow?"

Michael said, "That would be great. Is yours any good?"

"Excuse me? Well, if you don't like it, you don't have to smoke it."

I gave Tom a look like, *Who the hell does this guy think he is?* Tom could tell that I was getting a little agitated with his cousin.

"So, there's not much to tell," Tom said. "I filled you in with all the particulars up in Oregon. Do you have any questions?"

"Yes," I said. "How long does this whole process take? A month or two?"

Michael snorted a couple of lines of coke and passed the mirror to me. I just looked at it while waiting for his answer. I looked over at Tom and glanced back down at the mirror. I pulled the mirror closer to myself while looking up at Michael.

"This isn't an overnight and it's done sort of thing," Michael said. "This will take anywhere from four to six months to do it right."

I snorted a couple of lines while Michael continued to explain.

"First, I have to get a diamond ring for you. This is just a loaner for a day or two in order to give you enough time to take it to a jeweler and have it appraised. In the meantime, you go buy yourself a decent CZ that you can wear around so your friends can all see it. You will, of course, have to come up with a good story that sounds believable as to where and who you received this ring from." Michael stopped for a minute so he could do a couple more lines of coke as Tom and I passed a joint between us.

Michael continued, "I'm sure you have dated some married men, or at least some wealthier ones that you can build into your story. Every older man wants nice jewelry on the lady he's with. He wants everyone who sees her to know that she is spoiled and in turn, so is he. You can come up with a good story, can't you?"

"Yes, I can handle that," I said. "Now tell me about the police, and where do they come into all of this?"

Michael replied, "After a sufficient amount of time, like I said, four to six months goes by, and you will arrange to be gone one night when Tom will break into your apartment and supposedly steal the diamond ring. It's at that point when you call the cops to report a break-in, that they get involved. Now you're going to have to know your story inside and out, because they're going to quiz you on where this ring came from and they will want names. So, you better practice up on your acting chops. No screwing this up or we all go down."

Michael turned to Tom and said, "Are you sure she can handle this? She seems a little jumpy to me."

Tom assured Michael, "Yes, Judy can do this. I have faith in her."

"Well, I hope you're right because faith won't keep us out of jail; a good story teller will," Michael said as he looked me in the eyes, as if to send some sort of subliminal message like, *Don't screw this up, bitch*. Michael continued, "I'll get a ring to Tom that he'll bring you in the next day or so, and will go with you to have it appraised. We'll get this all set up before you head back to Oregon, Tom."

Michael finished snorting all the coke that was left on the mirror—a sizeable amount in my eyes. He packed up his mirror and tucked the hundred-dollar bill in his pants pocket.

He turned to Tom to say, "Tom, are you ready? You can always come back later if you want. Let's get going. I have some other business to tend to." Michael got up and started walking to my bathroom without even asking where it was. I thought that was a little odd, with a pinch of rude thrown in.

Needless to say, I really didn't like this guy too much. I turned to Tom and whispered, "What's with him? Does he think he's God's gift to the world?"

Michael came out of my bathroom and said, "It was nice meeting you. I'll be in touch. You follow the plan and everything will be just fine."

PRESENT DAY:

"Excuse me, ma'am? Would you like a drink? Another Rum and Coke?" asked one of the many cocktail waitresses, startling me, when all I could hear is Michael telling me to follow the plan.

I looked up at the waitress from my position on the floor and said, "Yes, two, please." I took the two glasses, setting one on the ground, and drinking the other.

What have I done? Michael is going to kill me. Sitting there drinking my Rum and Coke, I couldn't stop thinking about what Michael's reaction would be.

The man scares me. He had taken it upon himself a couple of times to just show up at my apartment for no apparent reason other than "he was in the neighborhood" and thought he would stop in to see how I was doing. He always seemed to have some coke with him. Whenever he would do this, I felt very uncomfortable with him. I didn't trust this man; he was just too shady.

Enough worrying about Michael, it was too late now that the deed was done. *I'll call Tom when I get home and talk to him about it instead of Michael. Now the question is, "What's next?" I suppose I should gather up my belongings and figure out what I'm going to do for the night.*

Even though it felt like it should be a lot later, it was only 2:30 pm.

I downed the second Rum and Coke, got myself up off the floor, grabbed my suitcase, and started to walk to the entrance of the casino, past the front desk and through the revolving doors to the Las Vegas strip out front. Once I got outside, I ran into the young gentleman that was so kind enough to give me a hug. He and his buddy were still hanging around, watching all the action.

"Hey, beautiful! How are you doing?" questioned Pete.

"I'm doing okay, I guess," I said. "I'm just not sure where to go or what to do between now and the time my flight leaves tomorrow."

Pete asked, "How long were you stuck up there? We heard that they are doing a triage of injured people at the Convention Center. Maybe we should take you over there and get you checked out. You were in there long enough to have some pretty gnarly smoke inhalation. It couldn't hurt. Then after that, if you feel comfortable enough with us, you are certainly welcome to spend the night at our apartment, and we can take you to the airport when it's time."

I replied, "I feel pretty good, but I suppose it wouldn't hurt to be looked at. I know my nerves are shot."

We walked to Pete's car and headed for the Convention Center. It was amazing to see so many volunteers and first responders there. They had cots lined up in rows. I had to check in at the front where they took all of my personal information, including where I was in the hotel and how long I was inside. Then, I was escorted to my own cot. They immediately gave me oxygen and took all my vitals.

After about ten minutes of oxygen, the nurse checked my levels again, and I must have needed it as she said,

"Your oxygen levels are looking much better now. You did get a bit of smoke in your lungs, but things sound okay, and I believe you should be just fine. Here is a Valium for your nerves. I am so very sorry. That must have been a horrifying experience to go through. Take it easy the rest of the day and you should be fine to fly home tomorrow."

With that said, we got up and walked out. Once we got to the boys' apartment, I felt a little more comfortable with them, as they lived there with their girlfriends. We all introduced ourselves, and they offered me a drink.

"Oh, thank you, but no. I've had enough to drink today that my liver is swimming," I said to them. "Are you 420 friendly? If so, I would love to smoke a joint." Jim replied, "We are very 420 friendly… we just don't have anything right now."

I went to my suitcase, opened it up, digging around for my baggie of weed.

"Found it. Not a problem, folks. I usually bring mine with me. I'll just roll us a couple of joints and I know I will feel much better. That Valium she gave me hasn't fazed me in the least." I pulled my lighter out of my purse and lit the two joints, passing them to the others.

The girls were busy in the kitchen making hamburgers to barbecue. By the time we ate and visited a while, it was about eight o'clock, and all I wanted to do was go lie down.

Pete showed me to their room and said, "You can sleep in our room. I know Gayla put clean sheets on the bed today. We can sleep on the couches."

I replied, "I don't want to put the two of you out of your own bed."

"No, we insist. You've been through quite a bit today. Make yourself at home and get a good night's sleep. We'll see you in the morning and get you to your plane on time. Good night."

Pete pulled the door shut all but about two inches. It was just enough that I could see the television from where I was lying. They had the volume turned down, but it was still loud enough that I could hear everything they were saying.

I laid on my left side, watching the news. It was the first time I really saw what was happening. I had a limited view from the hotel room on the thirteenth floor. This was showing the whole building with cameras in the sky filming, the helicopters plucking the victims off the roof one at a time. It also showed furniture being thrown out windows, that I had heard while I was in the building. This included the sounds of the smashing glass as a chair would go out a window, and the tinkling of shattering glass as they hit the ground. The people were screaming, muttering sounds that you couldn't make out. But you knew in your heart that they were crying for help.

They did not show it on the news, but they did mention one person had jumped to their death from one of the higher floors. I couldn't have done that. I would have gone out on my handmade rope, and at least given it my best shot to climb down as far as I could.

After the news started to repeat itself, I couldn't listen anymore. This had certainly been a very trying day. I think because of the sudden surprise of the building being on fire, I immediately went into survival mode. I didn't take the time to be scared; there wasn't time to be scared. There was just time to deal with the situation at hand as best you could to insure your survival.

I thought I was scared when I saw that headlight on the train coming straight at me, but this was different. This was imminent fear that I couldn't even wrap my head around. It was so massive to comprehend. All I could think of was, "I'm never going to see anyone I know or love again." But I couldn't allow myself to think that way. I had to be positive that we were getting out of there somehow, someway. If you had taken my blood pressure while I was in that room, it would have been off the charts. I certainly knew my pulse was high. I wished I had been; I would have been much calmer inside.

I realize today how close I came to dying.

That day, I prayed, *Thank you so very much, Angel Bob, for having my back today. I can't tell you enough about how grateful I am to be alive right now, and safe. Thank you so very much for protecting me and keeping me safe from harm. I love you very much. Thank you, thank you, thank you.* With that said, I rolled over, putting a pillow over my head, and fortunately fell fast asleep.

The next morning came quite quickly, it seemed. After fully waking up, I got dressed and went out to the living room. Everyone was awake; I hadn't realized it was almost 10 o'clock.

Pete was the first to speak. "Would you like some breakfast? Gayla just made some pancakes and bacon. Help yourself. How are you feeling today?"

"Good morning, everyone," I said. "I'm good, I got a solid night's sleep, and I'm ready to go home. I believe my flight leaves about one this afternoon. You can take me out to the airport whenever it's convenient for you. I don't mind sitting out there until it's time to leave."

"No, don't be silly," Pete said. "Get some breakfast, relax, smoke a joint, and don't you worry about a thing. We'll leave here about noon, that should give you plenty of time to get checked in and on your way." After eating breakfast, I went into the bathroom to get ready. It didn't take me long, as I was not in the mood to put on too much makeup. I just wanted to be home in my apartment. Once I was ready, we sat around watching sports and smoking until it was time to leave.

I don't remember too much about the ride to the airport except this one thing. We had to drive by the MGM Grand on the way to the airport. I remember looking at it and getting this very strange feeling. It was like looking at a ghost building. You knew no one was in there now and it made you think of all the lives that were lost just a mere twenty-four hours ago. It seemed like an eerie, quiet chill that came over me as we drove past. It was such a strange feeling, one that I will never forget. I have to hand it to Angel Bob. He definitely did his job the day before.

You will hear me speak quite a bit about Angel Bob throughout this series. He is my main guardian angel, who has watched over me my entire life. He's been quite busy. I do have to hand it to him, I am extremely glad to have Bob on my side. Trust me, I thank him daily for all that he has protected me from. Things that I have seen, and all the things that could have happened if Bob hadn't been there watching over me.

I read somewhere once that if you ask your guardian angel their name just as you are about to go to sleep, you will get an answer within ten days. Angel Bob only took four days. I remember waking up after the fourth evening of asking. I was still somewhat asleep, and all of a sudden, on the right side of my head, towards the top, I hear the name Bob. I shot up in bed, sitting there for a moment, and asked "Bob??? Really? Is your name Bob?"

For about the next two weeks, each night as I was going to sleep, I asked, "Is your name really Bob?" He has never answered that question, so all I can assume from that is that my guardian angel's name is truly Bob. Quite frankly, I really don't care what his name is. All I know is that he has done one heck of a great job protecting me in my lifetime.

I *personally thank you, Angel Bob, daily!*

I vaguely remember the airport or boarding the plane. I just remember finally arriving home. The first thing I did besides pet the cat was to call my mother. I wanted her to know that I was home safe and sound. I then called my boss to let her know that I was home, and also that I would not be into work for a day or two. I needed some time to get mentally straight again.

After that, I got into my comfy clothes, went to bed, and turned on the television. I wanted to sleep. I was not just physically worn out, but also mentally exhausted. I believe it was finally sinking in as to what exactly I had gone through. Other than the train hitting me, this was as close as I had ever come to death in my twenty-seven years. That was quite the ordeal that I had experienced, and hope to never experience it or anything like it again in my lifetime.

I slept in the next morning until past ten o'clock. I rolled over onto my back, staring at myself in the mirror above the waterbed for the longest time. *What am I going to tell Michael? When am I going to tell Michael? Maybe I'll wait until I see the insurance man and see what he has to say before I try to reach him.*

I was truly not looking forward to talking to him. I knew I did the right thing, but I also knew he was not going to be happy about it because I did not follow the plan. This made so much more sense to do it the way I did.

I laid there starring at myself, wondering, *Why the hell did I ever agree to do this? Was it the money? The excitement? Or was it the mere fact that Tom had suggested it, and in my mind, he could do no wrong? I don't know. I just know that I am really starting to regret this choice I made. I'm not a bad person; I just did something bad. Well, exceedingly stupid, anyway. Why did I ever agree to this, especially after meeting Michael? I tell you, the man scares me for some reason.*

That alone should have been a big red flag as a reason not to do this. But I was just looking at paying off my credit card after making my graduation costumes. I still should never have agreed. *I am truly sorry that I got involved with this.* But I did make the choice and now I had to finish it.

I went to the kitchen to get some breakfast—a bowl of Cheerios and my vitamins. After I finished, I rinsed off my dish and put it in the dishwasher. I knew I had to call Tom at some point and tell him what had happened. I noticed that I was wandering from room to room, puttering with something in each room. I was basically wasting time, putting off the phone call to Tom. I walked over to the phone, picking up the receiver, and dialing the insurance man's number. I knew I would only get his answering machine, but I wanted to let him know I was home.

"Hello, Harry, this is Judy Bohning calling. I wanted to let you know that I am back in town now. I am not going into work tomorrow, so if you'd like to see me, I'm free anytime. I look forward to your call. Goodbye."

I paced the apartment a few more times, sat on the couch, pulled out my smoke tray, and rolled a couple of joints, hoping that would help calm me down a bit. When I finished, I got up to get something to drink, then I started smoking the joint and wandering around the living room again. I hadn't realized how scared I was of Michael until now. He definitely gave the impression of always getting his way, and if he didn't, it would not be pretty.

In my mind, it made sense to do what I did. You could not fake the level of horror and fright I had at the time of the fire. That was real and I used it to my advantage. All right, after I finished the joint, it was time to sit down and tell Tom what I did. Hopefully, he wouldn't say anything to Michael until after I saw Harry on Monday. But I did need to tell Tom right away.

I went back over to the couch, picked up the other joint I had rolled, lit it, got the ashtray and my roach clip, then picked up the phone and dialed Tom's number. I was almost hoping he wouldn't pick up, but he did.

"Hello."

"Hi, Tom. It's Judy. Are you busy?"

"No, not at all. What's up?"

"Have you seen the news this week?"

"Did you hear about the fire at the MGM Grand in Las Vegas?"

"Yeah! Wasn't that something? I would have hated to be vacationing there this week."

"Well, I wasn't vacationing there, but I was there for work. I had a great view of the whole thing from the thirteenth floor. It truly was 'something.'"

Tom gasped. "Wait, what? You were there? What were you doing there? Did you take the week off or something?"

I responded, "No, I was there working. The costume house that I work for was doing the extra costumes for the new Bob Mackie show that was supposed to have opened last night. It was horrifying. I didn't think I was going to make it out for the better part of an hour or more. I knew right away that I only had two options. I could be a pancake or a marshmallow."

"What are you talking about?" Tom asked.

"I was stuck on the thirteenth floor for six hours. If there was fire coming through the door, I was going out the window on a rope I made from torn-up bed sheets. I was not about to burn. I would much rather have taken my chances that the firemen could reach me somehow, or they might have had one of those blow-up bags you fall on from high up. Who knows what would have happened, at least that had several different outcomes. Sticking around with fire, there were no options. The only option was a horrific, painful death. With the rope, if anything went wrong, I wouldn't feel a thing after the sudden stop. It would be quick and basically painless. And definitely dead from that height."

Tom replied, "Geez, Judy, I am really sorry you had to go through all of that. I would have gone crazy."

I chimed in, "Oh, there was a Canadian woman in our room who was going crazy. She was absolutely hysterical and knew we were all going to die. Yeah, she was a real hoot and a half."

Tom asked, "Are you all right? Other than being scared out of your mind."

"No, I'm okay," I responded. "It was just a little fire. I'm fine. I don't need to see anyone. I need to be alone for a couple of days before I go back to work."

Tom sounded happy to hear I was alright. "I'm glad you're okay. Glad you called, too. I wanted to talk to you about when I'll be coming down to take care of that little issue we have."

I took a deep breath, and a drag off the joint, to finally tell him, "Well, we need to talk about that."

Tom responded quickly, "What exactly does that mean? This doesn't sound good to me. What's up?"

"You don't know what it was like there," I said. "You have no idea what exactly I went through. By the time it was all over and I was out of the building, I was hysterical and very distraught. I tried calling Michael, several times, but he never picked up. So, I found it necessary to make an executive decision. I decided to call the insurance man and tell him that the diamond ring had been stolen off my dresser in my room with all the commotion that was going on. I was crying real tears and I made it sound very believable."

"You did WHAT?!?" Tom shouted. "Are you being serious right now? Because if you are, Michael is going to pitch a fit when he hears this."

I jumped right back in with, "It was the perfect thing to do. I was very upset, and I'm supposed to go into his office tomorrow to see him about everything."

Tom snapped: "I understand that you were upset at the time,

but you shouldn't have done anything before you talked with Michael. When do you plan to tell him?"

I hesitated a few seconds and said, "I was kind of hoping you could tell him. After all, he's your cousin. Plus, he may not yell as much at you because you're just the messenger. And I don't really feel like having him yell at me right now. I tell you, Tom, that man scares me."

He spoke right up: "Then why did you change things up and go against the plan? If he scared you before, you should be scared now. I'll tell him for you, but be prepared to have a visitor on your doorstep thirty minutes after I tell him. Because I'll tell you what he's going to do. He's going to get off the phone with me, get in his car, and drive straight to your place, where he will confront you. I just hope your walls are on the thick side."

My heart was pounding. "Well, please don't say anything to him about this until after I see the insurance man. That way, I'll be able to tell him it's being taken care of and there is nothing to worry about. It's been handled and no police."

Tom sounded grim: "I hate to tell you this, Judy, but once you see your insurance man, you will have to go down to the police department and fill out a report. So, you really haven't avoided anything, you've just got yourself in Dutch with Michael. And that will not be fun."

My heart pounded harder. "Well, do me a favor, and don't tell him until Tuesday. Please! By then I will have seen the insurance man, and I can at least give him an update as to what is happening. But, please, please, don't tell him until Tuesday. Then, when you do, would you please give me a heads up so I can know to expect him? I would really appreciate it."

Tom replied, "Yes, I will let you know after I talk with him. Just be careful, please."

"Thank you, Tom. I'll be careful. After all, he still gets his money. I really don't see what the big deal is. Okay. I gotta go. I'll give you a call tomorrow night to let you know how everything goes. Goodbye."

I hung up, really sorry that I chose to do this with them. But seriously, what was he going to do? He wasn't going to kill me, so I didn't need to worry about that, not for a couple of grand that he was going to get, anyway.

I rolled another joint and picked up the phone to call my girlfriend, Pamela. She is a fabulous jazz singer and model— beautiful, six-feet-tall, with platinum-blonde hair, cut short like Billy Idol's. She never made it to the top because she refused to play the casting couch game. So she wrote, produced, and recorded her own music.

Pamela answered the phone and we talked for a good hour. I told her all about my experiences; she even knew about the ring thing with Michael. I told her everything. She's like the big sister I always wanted. Pamela is a couple years older than me, but much wiser in the ways of the world. In other words, she can tell when someone is blowing smoke up her ass and she puts them in their place. I so admire her for her self-confidence and self-esteem.

I remember she told me one very important thing when I was going home for my ten-year class reunion. I was very nervous, because I had been so damn shy in high school, and I was afraid to talk to people. But Pamela said just one thing, "Judy, it's all attitude."

That was all I needed to hear. I kept repeating it to myself and made myself a knock-out outfit to wear. It was white gauze with black leopard print, a halter-top, and a diaper skirt that showed nothing but leg from the top thigh, down on each side. I walked into that reunion like I owned the place with Pamela's voice replaying in my head, saying: "It's all attitude. It's all attitude."

I must say, I did make an impression that night. In fact, the next night, I was voted "most changed." But you'll have to wait to hear how that weekend went.

Back to our phone call, Pamela had a suggestion: "Judy, after going through that fire and everything, girl, you need to see a psychiatrist. This is something that was very traumatic for you and will scare you for life if you don't talk to someone about it."

"Pamela, I don't need to see a shrink. I'm just fine. I'll get through this. There are just some loose ends that need to be tied up, and it's all over and behind me. I better let you go. I've talked your ear off long enough. Let's get together for drinks some night this week. Now, that, I could use."

"That sounds like a great idea. I'll give you a call in a couple of days. You have a good day, and take care of yourself. Talk to you later."

"Bye, Pamela." And I hung up.

I rolled myself another joint and went to my drawing table, taking a seat in my favorite chair. *I can't let this get to me today. I really don't understand what the big deal is.* The ring was stolen, that was the whole point. It was in the hands of the insurance man, and however long it took, we would be paid out. Why Michael would get upset over that was beyond me.

Besides, I always thought it was a little risky having Tom break into my apartment. I have so many neighbors; someone would have seen something and told the police. I was uneasy about that. Not as uneasy as the idea of going to the police station and filing a fraudulent police report. That alone was a crime, but, *Let's be real, Judy, it's not that big a deal compared to insurance fraud.* Either way, I was really regretting getting involved in this. It was just too shady from the beginning.

Sometimes I wondered what kind of hold Tom had on me. Just because he was the first man I ever willingly slept with, didn't mean I had to be in love with him. But I couldn't help myself. I *love him. He's the reason I walked out of the wedding to Howard three days before the nuptials.* Well, that and the fact that I was going to be an instant mommy to a five-year-old brat, and that he was cheating on me. I did the right thing by not marrying Howard.

I'm not doing the right thing now, but I'm in too deep, and there is no turning back at this point. I have to finish what I started. Then, I can forget that Michael ever existed.

I started drawing and smoking, both of which took my mind off my current circumstances. That was how I finished out my day. I did get quite a bit accomplished, which was good. I headed to the bathroom to brush my teeth and wash my face before crawling into bed. *I wonder if there's anything good on* TV?

I woke up early Monday morning. I did the usual things: pee, eat my Cheerios, and get into the shower. After which I proceeded to put on my makeup and do my hair, since I would be seeing Harry today. I was just finishing my hair when the phone rang. It was Harry.

"Good morning, Judy. How are you doing now that you're home and have had a few days to recoup from your ordeal?"

I replied, "I'm doing as well as I can. After it was all over, it hit me as to what I had just gone through. I'm still a little shaken by the whole thing, but better. Thank you."

Harry asked, "Can you come into the office today, about one o'clock?"

"I certainly can. I'll see you at your office this afternoon. Thank you, Harry, for helping me through this. I've never experienced anything like this before. I feel totally lost right now."

"Well, you just don't worry about a thing. We'll get this all taken care of as painlessly as possible. See you at one. Goodbye."

As 12:30 approached, I was getting more and more nervous. I sat down and rolled several joints, putting them in my little silver antique cigarette case I found at my friend's antique store in Beverly Hills some years back. It was time to leave.

I arrived and got parked about five minutes early. I could see Harry in his office as I approached the building. Now I was very nervous. I stopped for a second, opened my purse, and took out a Valium, popping it in my mouth, chewing and swallowing. They do taste rather bitter, but you get used to it when need be.

Harry must have seen me walking up the sidewalk, as he was in the reception area to greet me.

"Hello, Judy. You look very lovely today."

"Hello. Thank you."

"Let's go into my office," he said, motioning to his door with his right hand. Being the gentleman that he was, he waited for me to enter, then followed, closing the door behind him.

Once I was seated, he walked behind his desk and sat in his chair. He was looking for my file on top of his desk, scooping it up and opening it.

"I have pretty much done most of the paperwork I just have a few questions for you," he said. "Where was the ring the last time you saw it?"

"It was on the dresser with my watch and other jewelry," I said. "I had taken everything off and laid it out on the dresser, as I was going to take a shower that morning. Once I came out of the bathroom, my room was black, and that's when I realized there was a fire and I needed to get out. The only thing I was thinking about at that moment was getting dressed and getting the hell out of there. The jewelry didn't even cross my mind at that moment."

I looked straight at him, recounting my story with confidence. "After I was dressed, I went to the door, and upon opening it, I ran into a gal about my age, and her mother. They had come down from the sixteenth floor, but could only go as far as the twelfth floor, because the fire doors were locked. So, they came back up to my floor. The smoke was knee-high, and we had to do something, so we knocked on the door across from my room. There was a Canadian couple in there who were kind enough to let us in. The woman was hysterical and just knew we were all going to die. She was as fun as a porcupine in a balloon factory."

I continued, "We were in their room a good couple of hours before I felt comfortable enough to go back to my room to get my belongings. It was when I was throwing everything into my suitcase that I went over to the dresser to get my watch and the jewelry, and everything was gone."

I felt I was playing this role very well, because it was mostly true until this point. "I totally freaked out. I looked all over, and on the floor, to see if I had knocked them off. Nothing. They were nowhere to be found. I knew I couldn't take that long, so I grabbed my packed suitcase and went back across the hall to the room we were all in. And I never saw the ring or anything else again."

Harry asked, "Do you have any idea what might have happened

to them?"

I responded, "When I went back to my room to get my things, the door was ajar. It must not have shut all the way when I left. To be honest, I really wasn't concerned about much, other than getting the hell out of there. But, yeah, I remember not having to use my key to get in. The door just pushed open."

Harry asked, "About what time was this?"

My answer was, "It must have been about 9:30 or 10, I believe, when I went back to my room. And that's just a guess because my watch was with everything else."

Harry said, "I called the head office today to check on a police report to go along with the claim. In order to file a police report, you would have to go back to Las Vegas and file it with them, since the theft occurred in their jurisdiction. Now, I'm just assuming here that you really aren't in any hurry to return to Las Vegas?"

"No!" I exclaimed. "I really don't care to go back there anytime soon. So, what do we do about the police report?"

"Well," Harry said, "the head office said that it is such a major event that we really don't need a police report with this one. Especially since you would have to go back there to get one. No, we're just going to push this through without the report. Everything will be fine. You don't have to go back there any time soon."

I let out a big sigh of relief.

Thank you, Angel Bob, for this one. That is fabulous news.

Sounding somewhat upset and distraught I said, "Good, I couldn't go back to that town just yet. I think it's going to be a while."

A tear rolled down my cheek. Harry noticed and handed me a box of tissue. At the same time, he gave me the insurance paperwork to look over.

"Here you go," Harry said. "Look over the paperwork and see if it all looks in order to you. Then I need you to sign where the yellow arrows are. I'll get this FedEx'd to the main office this afternoon. Being the sort of case that it is, don't be surprised if someone from the company calls to ask questions. I'm not sure how long it will take to settle this; give it several weeks to a month, and we should be all done. You can go out and buy yourself a replacement ring."

I cast a relieved expression. "Oh, that's exactly what I'm going to do. I loved that ring. But it just won't be the same ring that Jeff gave me."

There really was no Jeff, that was just the name I gave to my secret admirer who supposedly gave me the ring. I never really talked about him to anyone. When someone would ask about him, I told them that he was rather high up in politics, and he was married, too, so I really didn't want to talk about him. That made it very easy to get out of that question. My private life was nobody's business.

I finished signing all the paperwork and handed it back to Harry.

He looked it over and said, "This looks like we have everything we need. You go on about your life, and you will be hearing from me when the check comes in. If you haven't heard anything in a month, give me a call and I'll check into it. We should be all settled in a few weeks' time. Hey, it was great meeting you, Judy. Now, don't worry about a thing, it's all done."

I couldn't wait to wrap this up. "Thank you for everything, Harry, especially for putting up with that hysterical phone call from Vegas. I've never been so scared in all my life. I'll look forward to speaking again. You take care, now."

Finally back in my car, I just sat back with a very big sigh of relief. *Thank goodness that part is over with.*

Oh, if Harry only knew what, or I should say who, I had to worry about. I really didn't understand now why Michael would be upset at all. Everything was working out. I didn't have to file a fraudulent police report. I'd say we, or I, got out of that fairly easy.

I got home and immediately got into my comfortable clothes. I was not just physically drained, but very emotionally drained. I had to watch every word that came out of my mouth when I was with Harry. I certainly didn't want to screw up in any way. Which, with my mouth, that could have happened very easily. Sometimes my mouth goes into gear before the brain can stop it from saying something I shouldn't.

It was about four o'clock by now, and I was thinking that I should probably call Tom and tell him how everything went. I walked over to my purse that was sitting on the kitchen counter to get my silver cigarette case out. I looked around the kitchen for a lighter, found one with the ashtray. I turned to get a bottle of Dr. Pepper out of the refrigerator, and opened it with the bottle opener that was hanging from the wall. I took everything over to the couch to settle in and call Tom. I picked up the phone, dialed his number, it rang about three times before he answered.

"Hey, Tom, it's all done. I just got home from the insurance company. I would say that I got off pretty easy, considering. They said we could go ahead and file the claim without a police report. However, I would have to go back to Vegas to file it with them since that was the jurisdiction where the ring was stolen. Harry said that because it was a well-known event, we could do without the report. Thank God!"

"Well, that's interesting that they are putting it through without a police report," Tom said. "I've never heard of that happening. You did get lucky. So, what did the guy say about the claim?"

"After all was said and done, he told me it should be just a few weeks before I get the settlement. That alone should make Michael happy. I just don't understand why he's going to be so upset about me doing what I did. I did try calling him several times, and he never picked up, so he can't blame me completely."

"Oh, I wouldn't think that way if I were you," Tom said. "Michael is going to be upset just because you didn't do what you were told. Don't be so naïve to think he won't."

I shook my head. "I don't get it. It's done, the insurance has been taken care of, and in a few weeks, he will have his money. How could he get upset about that? Everything worked out."

Tom popped up with, "All I'm saying is, don't be surprised if he blows his top. Michael likes it his way, and only his way. You don't know him that well, and I hope you never do. All right, I'll call him tonight to let him know that things have changed and where we are with everything. But I'm warning you, don't be surprised if he shows up at your door within the hour."

"He better call first," I warned, "because I'm so mentally exhausted that I'm going to bed now. If he does show up on my doorstep unannounced, I'm just not home tonight."

"Okay, Judy. You take care of yourself and I will talk to you later. Let me know when you hear from Michael."

"I sure will. You take care, too. Bye." I hung up, and took my ashtray and joint into the bedroom, putting them on my nightstand. I went back to the kitchen for a bowl of ice cream, and returned to the bedroom, crawling into bed.

I know it's early but I just want to hide in bed for the night and forget this all ever happened. I sure hope there is something good on TV to take my mind off of the here and now.

It was about nine o'clock when my phone rang. I must have fallen asleep because I was startled at the ring, and out of habit, almost answered the phone. I realized it could be Michael, and he was the last person I wanted to talk to. I let the answering machine answer it.

"Hey, Judy, it's Tom. I just wanted—" I picked up.

"Hey, Tom. So, how did it go?"

Tom replied, "Surprisingly well. He took it much better than I thought he would. I explained to him your situation and how you called the insurance man from there. I let him know that you went in to see the guy today about the claim. That it had been started, no police report was needed, and that it should be all settled in a few weeks. He didn't seem to flinch."

My response was, "That's good to hear. Maybe it's not going to matter at all as long as he gets his money. I know I haven't heard anything from him tonight."

Tom said, "And you won't. He and Marla are out at some charity function for her school."

Here's where it got interesting. Marla was really Tom's cousin by blood. He just called Michael his cousin, but it was only through marriage. So, Tom's loyalties really were with Marla. This will be important later.

My response: "Well, that's good to hear. Now I can get a good night's sleep before I have to worry about talking to him. But from what you've said, it sounds like it's not going to be a big deal. Which is good. I've been worried sick over how he was going to take this."

Tom said, "I wouldn't worry about it too much. He sounded pretty cool about the whole thing. Now smoke a joint and go to sleep. I'll talk to you later."

"That's exactly what I am doing. Thank you for calling and telling him what's happened. I was scared to death to tell him. I certainly appreciate it, Tom. You have a good night, and I'll talk to you after I hear from Michael. Good night."

I hung up in relief, at least for another twelve hours.

Morning seemed to come quickly. Even though I wasn't going into work today, I still got up, had my Cheerios, took my shower, and got dressed. I needed to work on the sketches for my free-lancing job designing lingerie. I had been drawing for a couple of hours when I wanted a Dr. Pepper. I got up from my drawing table, walked into the kitchen, and had just opened the refrigerator when I heard a knock at my front door.

Gee, I wonder who that could be? Okay, Judy! It's time to put your big girl panties on and pray to God you don't end up messing them. I hope it goes as well as Tom said.

I went to answer the door. I peeked through the little peephole and I was right, it was Michael. Opening the door I said, "Good morning, Michael. How are you doing today? Come on in."

I stepped aside so he could get past me and into the living room. He went ahead and took a seat on the couch, still not saying a word.

I asked, "Could I get you anything to drink? I don't have coffee, but I do have tea, if you would like?"

He responded, "Maybe a bottle of water. Where is your mirror?"

I came back from the kitchen with a Dr. Pepper and a bottle of water, noticing a vial of coke on the coffee table, and said playfully, "Oh, starting the morning off with a bang, are you?"

I went into my bathroom, brought out my flat mirror, and handed it to Michael. He proceeded to pour out some coke and chopped it up, drawing out lines, then chopping some more. He played with it for the longest time before he said anything. The silence alone was killing me. Watching him chop the coke with a single edge razor blade rather vigorously made me quite nervous. It was almost like I could hear him yelling at me with each chop of the blade. The coke was certainly fine enough to snort now, but he just kept at it angrily.

Finally, Michael spoke. "I hear you were in the MGM fire. Tom told me things were handled, and that you had taken care of everything. He no longer had to come down and break into your apartment."

Michael sounded a bit different now, his voice was a little rougher. "So, tell me what happened. And don't leave anything out. I've got all day."

The way he said that sent a chill down my spine. I could feel the goosebumps running up my arms and the little hairs on the back of my neck standing up. He pushed the mirror over in front of me and said, "I left you the fat line. I figure you might need it. And if you have some joints rolled, they may come in handy, too."

I reached for the drawer to the end table, opening it, and pulled out my silver cigarette case. I had about five joints already rolled in it. I pulled out the fattest joint I saw and lit it up. After taking a drag, I handed it to Michael, and in turn, he handed me the rolled up hundred-dollar bill he loved to snort his coke with. I went ahead and hit the line, not taking it all.

"I figure I'll leave some for later," I said. "Don't want to waste it."

"Go ahead, do it all," Michael insisted. "There's more where that came from."

"No, thank you. I know my limits, and what I snorted was sufficient for now. I'll finish the rest in a bit." I then began to tell Michael the whole story about the fire.

"I tried calling you about a dozen times to talk to you about it, but you never picked up the phone," I said. "I was hysterical and distraught. I had to make a decision then and there, so I chose to call Harry, the insurance man. I was in tears and extremely upset. I couldn't have faked it as well if it had come to that. This was the best thing to do. I saw the opportunity and I took it. Everything has turned out for the best. The claim is being taken care of, and I'll have the insurance check in a few weeks. It all worked out. Everyone is happy. Right???"

I got up and asked him if he would like some more water.

He didn't answer.

I walked into the kitchen; it was long and narrow with only one way in and out. Next thing I knew, I turned and Michael was standing in that only way in and out. The light coming through the window behind him made him look like a very large shadow looming over the kitchen, very daunting.

We stood there for what seemed like an eternity, just staring at one another. He then put his hands on the countertops to each side of him. It gave me the feeling of a small animal being trapped with no way out. I tried to remain calm. Opened another Dr. Pepper for myself, took a sip to break the awkwardness.

Michael began to speak in a deeper voice than he normally does, and rather sternly, too.

"You do realize the problem at hand that we have here since you decided to go rogue on us, don't you? This was to be a three-way deal, but with what you just went and did, it takes away Tom's part in this. He has no apartment to rob. Now I have to decide if he should get paid his share or not because he didn't do anything. This puts me in a very precarious position. And I don't like being in precarious positions."

He took a breath while staring at me the whole time. "I suppose the right thing to do here would be for you and me to split Tom's share. I'll have to think about this while we're waiting on the check to arrive. So, a few weeks before we see a check? Please be sure to answer my phone calls. It's a bit of a drive into Studio City from Calabasas. I don't want to make it if I don't have to. I'll be the one to tell Tom about what I decide to do when I'm ready. So don't go saying anything to him about what we just talked about. Are we straight on that?"

I responded with a quiver in my voice. "Yes, I understand. But to be fair, Tom did have a part in all of this and should still get his share. If it wasn't for Tom, you and I would never have met, and we wouldn't be doing this right now. So, as I see it, Tom still should be paid his fair share. But I won't say anything."

Michael replied, "That's right, you won't. Remember that!"

He backed up and headed to the couch. He picked up his hundred-dollar straw, leaving the coke. He didn't even bother to say goodbye, he just walked to the front door, opened it, and was gone with a slam. I took that as a punctuation on our conversation. I was glad he was gone. It went better than I had thought, but that last little bit did put the fear of God in me. Very intimidating!

I don't like him. I never have and I never will.

I went over to the coffee table, where he had left the vial of coke.

I might as well have a snort. That and a joint might help calm the nerves.

I was quite surprised Michael left such a sizeable amount of coke. It had to be close to a gram. I thought that was rather odd. I snorted a couple of small lines, cleaned up the mess, and slid the mirror with the coke vial and razor under the couch. I picked out a joint from the case and went back to my drawing table, thinking that would relax me enough to call Tom without saying anything I shouldn't.

I looked up from my drawing and noticed that it was already 5:30 in the afternoon. *I should probably go call Tom and get that over with*. Little did I know that Michael had already spoken with Tom.

I did not learn this following information for another five years, as Michael was in the process of making sure that Tom and I never spoke to each other again. While Michael was scaring me to the point of not wanting to talk to Tom, he was loading Tom full of lies about me becoming a coke whore, especially after the insurance settlement. Supposedly, instead of paying off my bills, I snorted it all up my nose, and was even willing to sleep with Michael if he would hook me up with some when I ran out of money.

It wasn't until after my mother's death five years later that Tom and I did speak again. I'll share all of that when I tell you about the Palomino Club days while I was caring for my mother, who had liver cancer. When she passed away, Tom was the only one I really wanted—needed—to talk to at that moment in my life. So, I broke the five-year silence and called his number. To my surprise, it had been disconnected.

Now what? Wait, I believe I have his mother's number. So I called his mother. You'll have to wait for this story to find out what happened after I did get in touch with Tom.

I went to the living room and picked up the phone to call Tom. When he answered, he sounded a little strange. I couldn't quite put my finger on it.

"Hello," Tom answered.

"Hi, Tom, it's me. How are you doing?"

"I'm fine. So did you talk with Michael yet?"

"Yes, he came over this morning, about 10 o'clock. He acted strange when I opened the door for him. Didn't bother to say hi, just walked over to the couch, sat down, and pulled out his coke. He certainly seemed in a hurry to do some. Anyway, he asked what happened in Vegas, and I told him exactly what I told you. I thought he was going to start yelling or something, but other than the bit of intimidation I got from him, I thought it went rather well."

Tom replied, "I don't know if I'll be coming down now or not, since there is no need to break into your apartment. Michael said he would bring my share of the money up to Oregon, so I don't need to bother with the drive."

"Really!" I said rather surprised. "So, when will I be seeing you again?"

"I don't know. Probably not until you come up here again. You know how much I hate LA. If I don't need to, I'm not coming down."

"Well, okay then," I said. "I really don't know what to say. I know I'll be up for Christmas. Maybe I'll see you then? Feel free to call anytime if you'd like to talk."

"Yeah, sure. I need to get going. I have some people to meet. You take care. Bye," Tom said, somewhat quickly.

"Okay. Bye." I hung up, thinking that was a fairly strange phone call. Tom didn't sound like the Tom I spoke to yesterday. Something was wrong, but I don't know what. I tried not to let it bother me, but I couldn't help but think about it. What had Michael said to him? Apparently, he was going to get his money, so that was good.

Several days went by without hearing a word from anyone. I went back to work at the costume house. Friday rolled around and I got off work about 4:30. I headed home, stopping at the grocery store to pick up a few things. By the time I made it home, it was going on 5:30.

I played a message on my answering machine: "Hello, Judy, this is Michael. I want to stop by tonight and see how you're doing. Give me a call when you get this." Then it went to the dial tone.

I put everything away, rolled a joint, and sat on the couch. I *am really not in the mood to see Michael tonight, or any other night, for that matter.* But I remembered what he said the last time he was here, that I had better return his phone calls.

So, I smoked my joint with my cat, Turkey. Turk is a long-haired, half-Persian and half-Angora cat, all white. He is beautiful and is my best friend. He also loves to smoke, but he is picky. He only likes the good stuff. His favorite position to lay is on top of the couch, right above my right shoulder. He gets the best hits there. This time, however, he was laying in my lap, sensing that something was bothering me. In fact, he didn't like Michael, either. Turk always comes out to see who is here, but when Michael was over, he went into the bedroom, and would stay in there until Michael left. It was the strangest thing.

I reached for the phone and called Michael. He answered, "Hello."

"Hello, Michael, it's Judy. I just got home. What's up?"

"I'm going to be in the Valley tonight and want to stop in on you, see how you're doing. Just chat. I should be there about seven. Does that work for you?"

"Yeah, that's fine. I'll be home all evening. I have no plans for tonight except relaxing."

"Great. I'll see you at seven-ish." Michael hung up.

That was another thing that really annoyed me about him. I

can't stand it when someone hangs up the phone without some sort of acknowledgment of the call ending. A simple "bye" works.

Seven o'clock finally rolled around, and about five after, I heard a knock at my door. I checked the peephole and it was Michael. I opened the door and actually got a "good evening" out of him.

"Well, good evening to you, as well. Come on in. A bottle of water for you, or would you care for something else?"

"The bottle of water will be just fine, thank you," he said as I headed to the kitchen. D*id I hear him right? Did he just say thank you?*

I was shocked. That made me suspicious that he was up to something. I *will definitely be on my guard tonight*. I returned to the living room with his water, and a Dr. Pepper for myself. Once again, there was a vial of coke on my coffee table. He need not say anything. I reached under the couch and pulled out the mirror with the razor blade on it. I had put away the other vial of coke that he left here. As far as I was concerned, he could think that I did it all.

I set the mirror on the coffee table and slid it over to him. He was sitting at one end of the couch and I was at the other. I wanted to keep as much distance between us as possible.

"Thanks," he said. "How did you know?"

"When haven't you used it whenever you come over?" I asked.

He poured out a sizeable amount of coke and started his routine of chopping and playing with it. This time was different; he didn't seem as menacing as the other day. And it didn't take long for him to spread out several lines. He took out his trusty hundred-dollar bill as a straw and snorted a couple of lines.

Then he slid the mirror in my direction. I did just one line, as they were rather large and I really didn't like to overdo it. That racing-heart feeling was not my idea of a good time. Now, if I had some work that needed to get done, that was a different story. But to do it recreationally, just a dab would do.

Michael spoke up: "Why not do both lines? You don't have to worry about me running out; there's plenty."

"No, thanks. A little at a time is fine with me."

I reached for a joint in the ashtray and lit it, passing it to Michael. He seemed like a different person tonight, calmer and even nice. He wanted to hear more about my experience in the fire. Like he really cared. We talked about random stuff.

I finally asked him, "Have you talked to Tom this week? When I spoke to him last, he seemed a little distant. Is everything okay with him? You are still giving him his share of the money, aren't you?"

Michael answered, "Yes, I spoke to him a couple of times this week. He's just going through some stuff with school. He's decided to drop out of his Master's program."

"What?!? Are you serious? He only has to finish one class and he's done. Is he crazy? What in the world is he thinking?" Tom had wanted to finish this for quite some time, and to walk away from it now was insane.

"Yeah, we had a lengthy talk about it the other night. I tried to talk some sense into him, but he has his reasons and he's not sharing. He's just pissed off at the world right now," Michael said. "He seems to think that running coke is a little more lucrative work for him at the moment."

"You are still giving him his share of the money, aren't you?" I asked.

Michael came back with, "Of course, I am. Like you said, even though he didn't have to break in, he still got us together. He can use the cash right now."

"I'm fuming over the fact that Tom has decided to walk away from his Master's and run coke," I said. "He's much more intelligent than that. What is the man thinking? I don't want to talk about him anymore." Michael and I were still up at midnight doing more coke and smoking.

Next thing I knew, he was saying, "Why don't you scoot down to this end of the couch and we won't have to slide the mirror back and forth?"

"No, thank you. That's not necessary. I'm fine right where I'm at."

Michael started to slide down to my end.

I got up. "Look, Michael, I don't know if it's the drugs we've done tonight, or what. But I have absolutely no intention of doing anything with you."

"It's just a little fun. I won't tell anyone."

I came back with, "That's not the point. First of all, you are married and to Tom's cousin. Secondly, I am in love with Tom, and I am certainly not about to have an inappropriate affair with you. So just get that through your head and we will finish off what we started, then go our own ways."

I paused for a couple of seconds, then said, "Now, I think it's time for you to go. It's been a very long day and I am no longer in the mood for company. So, please, could you leave now? I would certainly appreciate it."

Michael, being the gentleman that he was pretending to be tonight, started to gather his belongings and put them in his man-purse. He got up from the couch, walking towards me. I stood my ground and he went in for the "good night" hug.

I reciprocated, but on the light side and quick. I backed off and started to head for the front door to let him out. I opened the door saying, "Thanks for coming over tonight. I got a chance to see the private side of you, not just the business side. Drive safe going home."

Michael walked down the hall to the door and tried to give me a kiss, but I turned my face in time for him to hit the cheek.

"You take care of yourself, now," he said. "I'll be checking in on you from time to time. Good night." And with that, he turned and walked down the hallway of my building.

I closed and locked the door, not really knowing what to think of all that went on tonight. Was he being nice just to try and get in my drawers? That was the most likely scenario, mainly because he was a sleezeball, no matter how nice he tried to be. I walked back to the couch to clean up the coke mess, and to my surprise, Michael left a gram bottle of coke on the mirror again. Well, at least I didn't have to pay for it. Not right now, anyway.

I cleaned off the mirror and slid it back under the couch, taking the new vial of coke into my bedroom and putting it in my hiding spot. Someplace no one would ever look. I went back out to the living room, picking up the bottles of water and soda, generally tidying up a pinch.

Gee, I'm not surprised I just did who knows how much coke this evening. I might as well light a joint and go draw for a while. I'm certainly not going to sleep for several hours, so let's be productive.

I headed into my workroom, turning on my music very low, and sitting at my drawing table to work on the lingerie line. Before I knew it, it was getting light out. It was time to try and get some sleep. Thank goodness it was Saturday, so I could sleep all day if I care to.

I'm really a night person. That is when I do my best work, but right now, it was time to head to bed.

I went into the bedroom. Turkey was asleep on my pillow as I crawled in bed with him. I reached over and took the phone off the hook. I planned to sleep today.

The next week came and went. Nothing out of the ordinary happened. I didn't expect to hear from Harry for another week or so. Michael has been quiet this week, thank goodness.

But it would sure be nice to hear from Tom. I know he's got issues right now, but he could at least call and talk about what's going on with him. This is just too strange for him to not call like this. But, I'm not about to call him. I'm too pissed at him right now for fucking up his Master's. There's got to be a good reason. He wouldn't just walk away for nothing.

Before I knew it, the week had flown by and it was Saturday morning again. I needed to finish that lingerie line—a couple more sketches and it was complete, ready for delivery and payment. About 10:30, the phone rang. I went into the living room to answer it.

"Good morning," Michael said. "How was your week?"

"Hello. It was uneventful. How was yours?"

Michael responded, "About the same as yours. So, are you going to be around later this afternoon, say about four-ish?"

"Yes, I'll be here. I have no plans for the night. I finished the freelance job I was working on, so I plan on being a slug this weekend. Sure, come on over."

"Okay, I'll see you then. Bye." With that, Michael hung up.

I didn't have to do much to get ready for him. I cleaned the kitchen and tidied the living room. As for myself, I didn't do anything. I had on my jeans and a t-shirt, with not a stitch of makeup. My hair was up in a bun. I had absolutely no intention of getting dressed up for this man.

Four o'clock rolled around and there was Michael's knock at my door. As always, I looked through the peephole and opened the door.

"Come on in," I said.

Michael took his same seat on the east end of the couch, while I continued around to the kitchen for his bottle of water and my Dr. Pepper. By the time I got back into the living room, Michael had found the mirror under the couch and had already poured out a pile of coke. He went into his chopping routine as I set the bottle of water on the coffee table near him.

"Thank you," Michael said.

Wow, another "thank you" out of him. He was really trying hard to play the nice guy. My guard went up immediately. *I don't care what he says or how hard he tries, there is no getting into these drawers tonight, or ever.* In fact, as I was getting ready, I took precautions and put in a Tampon. This way, I could tell him I was on my period if he tried anything.

Michael has the lines all laid out in a row. He took a couple of rather large hits and passed the mirror to me as he handed me his hundred-dollar straw. I took a couple of small hits. I wanted to keep my head on straight tonight. I didn't trust this man. I lit a joint, taking a couple of drags, and passed it to Michael. We started talking about things in general, politics, religion, art; we covered it all, it seemed.

Then, I asked my usual question, "Have you talked with Tom this week at all?"

Michael answered, "No, I haven't heard from him."

When in actuality, he had talked to Tom several times and was starting to tell Tom that I was beginning to do quite a bit of coke. Michael told him that every time he left my apartment, I had him leave me a gram. He also told him I had been going through a gram in about four days.

No wonder Tom was mad at the world, when he was really mad at me for supposedly getting into coke. This was why he hadn't called me. But I didn't find this out for five years. That was how long Tom and I went without speaking to each other. We had known one another since we dated my first year of college. We were in touch at least several times a year and I would always see him when I went home to visit my parents.

Michael said, "I don't know what it is you have for Tom, but if I were you, I would get over it. He's not in love with you. If he were, you would be hearing from him on a regular basis. That certainly isn't happening now."

I responded, "Then why, when I was up in Oregon in June, did he tell me he wanted me to have his baby? If he wasn't in love with me, he wouldn't be saying things like that. Tom only says what he means."

"Oh, Judy," Michael said, while going for another line of coke. After snorting it, he continued, "Don't be so naïve. How often does he come down to see you? If he cared, he would be down here more. Actually, he is down here fairly regularly when he's doing a coke run. Doesn't he see you then?"

"I'm not being naïve," I said. "I know he cares for me. And I have been in love with him since we met nine years ago. I see him every time I go home to visit my parents. I wasn't, however, aware of the coke runs he was making down here. Getting it from you, was he?"

Michael replied, "Oh, yeah, he's down here about every two months. He doesn't even call you? If not, I would say that's a good sign that he's just not that into you. Forget about him, Judy. He hasn't amounted to anything yet. Now that he's dropped his Master's, he's not going to amount to much. Face it, Judy, he's a loser, and the best thing for you to do is move on."

By now a tear was trickling down my left cheek. Michael had me very upset, but I didn't really want him to see me like this. I wiped it away before he saw it. I just sucked it up.

"Could we change the subject, please?" I asked.

Michael scooted closer to me to comfort me and let me know life would be all right. He caught me off guard by doing this and my reaction was to just let him hug me. It felt good to get some affection. All of a sudden, I realized what was happening. I pulled away.

"Thank you for the hug," I said, "but we best leave it at that. In fact, it's getting late and I need to unwind and get some sleep. It would probably be best if you left now."

Michael said, "I hate to leave you upset. Are you sure you would prefer to be alone now?"

"Yes. I will be just fine, thank you."

Michael gathered his goodies, putting them in his man-purse. *Those things are so ridiculous.* But he had to be hip and fashionable at all times. He gave me a hug goodbye and headed for the door. I was right behind him. He leaned in for a kiss, and I backed off and politely declined. He left. I closed and locked the door, and picked up the mess again.

Why does he continue to leave me grams of coke?

It was so unnecessary. Heck, I still had a full gram from the last time he was here.

For the next couple of weeks, Michael called on a regular basis to see if I had heard anything from Harry. He also stopped over a couple more times. I was getting very tired of his visits. All he seemed to want to talk about was Tom and how I needed to forget about him.

Finally, Harry called. "Hi, Judy, this is Harry."

"Hello, Harry. How are you? Is there news by chance?"

Harry said, "Yes, I just happen to have a check for you sitting on my desk. When would be a good time for you to come pick it up?"

"Well, let's see. This is Monday. I'm off work this week for the holidays, and I'm going home to Medford to see my parents. Is about 10 o'clock tomorrow good for you?"

"Ten tomorrow morning is fine. I will see you then. Goodbye, Judy."

"Yes, you will," I said. "Thank you very much for the call. You have a fabulous day. Goodbye, Harry."

Wonderful! I can pick up the check, get it cashed, and have this whole thing behind me by tomorrow night. Oh, what a fabulous feeling that will be. I'll be able to pay off my credit card, too. That's going to be the best.

The next morning, I was up bright and early to shower and do my hair and makeup. I picked out one of my favorite silk blouses. It had a deep purple paisley print with puffy long sleeves and a ruffle cuff. Ruffles ran down the center front, covering up the buttons. Slipping on my tightest jeans, I then tuck in the hem of the blouse and gave it a little tug to slightly hang over the black belt. On went the black, ankle-high cowboy boots/shoes. I was ready to finish what I started.

I drove to Harry's office, parking in the back lot. I walked in and approached the receptionist.

"Hello, Judy Bohning to see Harry."

The receptionist responded, "Have a seat. I will let him know you are here."

A couple of minutes passed as I got more nervous.

Oh crap, I *forgot to take a Valium*. I reached into my purse and popped a Valium real quick, chewing and swallowing. I really didn't like the bitterness of it, but it did the job. A few more minutes passed, then Harry came out of his office.

"Hello, Judy. How are you doing this morning? You look beautiful, by the way."

"Why, thank you very much. I needed to hear that." I took a seat across from him at his desk, setting my black Coach shoulder bag on the back of the chair.

Harry started by saying, "I am rather surprised at how quickly the head office took care of this for you. It usually takes several more weeks. I guess it was the fact that the fire was a national tragedy."

"Yes, I agree. Not that this has ever happened before, but I was expecting to wait a month or two. I certainly appreciate you doing everything you did to push this through. The sooner I can put this horrific event behind me, the happier I'll be."

Harry nodded. "I agree. Let's get this over with so you can move on. Here is a letter for you to sign saying you received the cashier's check from me. I will make you a copy of it for your records. And here is the cashier's check for $9,500. It's been very interesting doing business with you, Judy. If you ever need any type of insurance again, maybe after you replace the ring with another one, we should get that one insured."

I answered, "Thank you, Harry. Yes, once I replace the ring, I will be back to cover it. I guess you just never know what could happen to you from day to day. I certainly appreciate all your hard work. Thank you for your kind words to me that horrible day on the phone. You were comforting and that means a lot to me. Thank you again."

I stood, putting the letter and check into my purse, then placing the purse on my right shoulder. I reached to shake Harry's hand in a final thank you. I turned, walked out of his office, and to my car.

From there, I went straight to my bank to cash the check. Fortunately, I had no issues whatsoever with them. Thank goodness they didn't ask me to fill out any forms for the IRS. Being under ten grand, that wasn't necessary. I finished with the bank, tucked the money in my purse, and out to the car I went. I couldn't get home fast enough to get this money safely stashed away.

I parked my car and headed up to my apartment without even stopping to check the mail. In I went, and back to my bedroom. I had an antique commode I bought when I was living in Portland. It had a rounded metal plate in the back of the cupboard with a space behind it. That's where I hid my personal items, such as money and coke. I first counted out the money one more time on the bed, making sure it was $9,500 exactly. I placed all the hundred-dollar bills back in the envelope and stashed it in the commode.

I went to the kitchen to get a Dr. Pepper from the fridge, taking it over to the couch with the phone.

I called Michael.

"Hello, Michael. It's Judy. I wanted to let you know that I saw Harry today and picked up the check. I got it cashed as well, so you can come over anytime to pick up what you need."

Michael responded, "That's great. Were there any problems?"

"No. Everything went very well. No questions from anyone."

Michael piped up with, "How does six-ish sound to you?"

"Six will be fine. I'll see you then. Bye."

Six o'clock was fast approaching. Unfortunately, I looked fairly good today because I had curled my hair and put on makeup to see Harry. I didn't like looking good around Michael. I just didn't feel safe with him. But now that the money was here and he would be picking up two thirds of it for him and Tom, I hoped that should make him happy. I seriously didn't think I had anything to worry about tonight. It was all over with… done.

I can finally say "good night" to him and never have to see him again. Thank goodness.

I can put this horrible chapter behind me. I know I did something that was not right, and I do really regret it. Not because I had to deal with Michael, but because it was wrong. I don't know what I was thinking when I agreed to do this. I must have been out of my mind. Tonight, it's done, and I can move on and try to forget about everything.

I went into my bedroom to change into some looser fitting jeans, hanging my good pair in the closet, as well as my silk blouse. I then looked for an oversized t-shirt to go with it. No shoes, just socks, what I call my fuzzies. In the bathroom, I brushed out the curls in my hair and pull it up into a bun.

Right at six o'clock, Michael knocked on the door. I, as usual, looked through the peephole and opened the door.

"Good evening, Michael. How are you doing today?"

"I'm doing very well. Thank you."

I let him go first, walking into the living room. Michael headed for the couch and I kept going past him to the kitchen for the usual. I went back to the living room, setting Michael's water on the coffee table. I continued around to my end of the couch and sat down. Michael, of course, was chopping up his coke as he said, "I thought we would celebrate tonight. I brought a little extra coke with me. Feel free to pull out a joint."

I guess we had become a rather predictable pair, Michael with his coke and me with my joints. He took his two large hits and slid the mirror over to me. I picked up the hundred-dollar straw and snorted a couple of lines after passing the joint to Michael.

"So, did you get all hundreds?"

"Oh... that. Yes, I did. Let me go get it so we can get that part out of the way. I want to be done with this."

I walked to my bedroom to retrieve the envelope with the cash. I brought it out, handing it to Michael.

"Here you go. Please count it. It's all there."

Sure enough, that was exactly what he did, after he took another large snort of cocaine. He slid the mirror out of his way and started counting the money on the coffee table, putting it neatly into thousand-dollar piles. When he finished, he picked up three of the piles, setting them aside, then he picked up the pile with five hundred in it and handed all of that to me.

"Here is a little more than your share," he said. "I figured I'd just round it up. After all, you did the hard parts. Thirty-five hundred. Don't spend it all in one place."

"Thank you, Michael. So does that little extra come out of your share, or Tom's?"

"Don't be a smart ass, just take the money."

"Thank you."

I got up, taking my share into the bedroom, and returned to the couch.

We spent a good couple of hours talking. As usual, I asked him, "Have you by chance heard anything from Tom?"

Michael responded, "I called him after I spoke with you to let him know I would be up this weekend to deliver his money."

"Good. I'm glad you're giving him his rightful share. He does deserve it."

"Oh, he'll get every penny he deserves, alright."

"I've got to go to the bathroom. I'll be right back," I said, getting up off the couch, walking first into the kitchen to put my empty Dr. Pepper bottle away. I then headed for the bathroom, and before I knew what was happening, Michael came up behind me, grabbing the top of my right arm very forcefully with his left hand, enough to leave a nice bruise.

He swung me around, facing him.

He smacked my face!

The back of his right hand across my right cheek hit with stinging force.

It knocked me to the floor.

I was in total shock! *What the fuck just happened?* He got me good enough to stun me, as I lay there trying to comprehend what was going on.

Michael said in a very deep, mean voice, "That's for not following the plan." As he dropped to the floor, straddling over me, I looked into his dark eyes, and they seemed deep, empty, and pure evil.

I was starting to realize what was happening, but before I could move, he said, "And this is just because I can!"

He reached down, yanking the button of my jeans, opening and pulling them down to my knees with my panties.

As he undid his pants, I started to struggle, but he pinned my hands together with only one of his massive hands.

Next thing I knew, he was penetrating me with his very large penis. I was dry, and he was pounding me mercilessly. I could feel my skin tear. He was on top of me for what seemed like forever.

Since this had happened before, I closed down, hoping for a quick end. My eyes were shut so tight, I could feel my face clenching up at the same time as both my fists.

Do I dare try hitting him when he is finished? No, it would only get me more beat up.

When he finished, he pulled out, leaving his drippings to run down my inner thigh to the carpeting.

As he stood up, he said in a menacing tone: "And don't even think about telling anyone about this, or something just might happen to Tom." He pulled his pants up, fastening them and tucking in his shirt. He walked to the coffee table, gathered his things, and was gone in a flash.

The front door slammed shut.

He's gone, thank God.

I was left laying halfway between the doorway to the living room and the hallway. I curled up in the fetal position, wrapping my arms around my knees, rocking back and forth. I started crying and I couldn't stop sobbing.

The shock of what Michael just did to me, along with everything else, hit me at the same moment. How close I came to death at the MGM. If I had died there, tonight never would have happened. The insurance fraud that Tom got me involved in, and now the true side of Michael had come out. No wonder Tom said something about hoping that I didn't get to know him very well.

Now I know the man for who and what he really is… Evil!

After about fifteen or twenty minutes on the hallway floor, I finally got up. My face was as red as a beet, my eyes were swollen and puffy and very red from crying so much. I was trying to stop from sobbing. My breaths were deep and long.

I headed to the shower, removing my pants and top on the way. Under the stream of water, the sobbing resumed.

I couldn't wash myself enough to wash away the stank left from Michael. Now what? I leaned against the front of the shower with my hands on either side and my head bent forward as the hot water hit the back of my neck, running down my spine.

I couldn't call the cops because I had just committed a crime with this man. I couldn't tell anyone because Marla would find out and I didn't want to be the reason for her marriage to break up. I couldn't tell Tom because he would literally kill Michael, not just for raping me, but also for doing Marla wrong.

I've just got to put my big girl panties on and suck it up. Go on with my life as if nothing has happened. No fire, no insurance fraud but most of all… no Michael.

I was feeling so violated with nothing I could do about it. I spent the next two days in bed. I didn't answer my phone; I put a note on my door asking to please not disturb. I was too depressed and felt so lost, I couldn't get up and do anything other than feed Turkey. I laid there eating ice cream and watching trash TV, just to keep my mind off what happened the night before.

Interesting note, Michael did not leave any coke behind this time.

I knew it—all these weeks he was just baiting me. What an ass!!!

I never care to see or hear from him again. As far as I'm concerned, he can go straight to hell, and probably will.

On the third morning, I was lying in bed on my back, looking up at myself in the mirror. I needed to snap out of this funk. I had to pack because tomorrow, Saturday, I would fly home for the holidays, and to have my two upper wisdom teeth pulled. I was not looking forward to that.

It just so happened that my dad went in for exploratory surgery on Monday, December 22nd, 1980, the same day I would have my teeth pulled. Mom had told me that Dad was having stomach issues all summer and the doctors couldn't figure out what was wrong with him. That was the reason for the surgery.

I got out of bed, reached into my commode, and pulled out a vial of coke. I figured since I had so much to do today, it would be good to have some help. Besides, it would help me not think about Michael and what just happened.

I went into the living room to retrieve the mirror, bringing it back and setting it on the bed. I pulled open the drawer of the commode and found a straw. I poured out a little coke, enough for a couple of lines. After chopping and snorting those two lines, I put everything back, and wiping off the mirror, returned it to the bathroom.

I knew I was doing this not to forget about what happened, but to dull the pain of what happened. Right now, that was just fine with me. Anything to forget about Michael and what he did to me for just a few hours. Maybe tomorrow I could enjoy a few hours, then hopefully days, without thinking of it. Then longer and longer, until this gets stuffed away in my memory as deep as the other rape at age eighteen had, and I wouldn't think about it or him again.

I removed my t-shirt and got in the shower, washing my hair and every part of me again in hopes that I could wash away any part of Michael that might have been left. After the shower, I got dressed and looked in my closet for my suitcase. I put it on the bed and opened it, then started to pull out clothes that I would need up north.

The trip home and the weekend went in the blink of an eye. Before I knew it, it was Monday morning and my brother Richard had taken me to the dentist to have my wisdom teeth removed. He picked me up after my appointment and we headed to the hospital to see how Dad's surgery went.

I saw Mom in the hallway outside of Dad's room. I asked her, "So, what's wrong with Dad? Did they find out anything?"

"We'll talk about this at home," Mom quipped.

"Come on, Mom. You must know something. What is wrong with Dad?"

Mom walked off, heading towards the elevator. My Aunt Harriet, whom we call Aunt Hat, was there as well. She walked with me and my brother, who was following up in the rear as we all walked behind my mom. Not a word was said in the elevator on the way to the ground floor. Mom and Hat went towards Mom's car, and Richard and I went to his car.

We all arrived at the house, gathering around the dining table. I was very concerned because I had never seen my mother act like this before. Finally, she spoke up: "Your father has pancreatic cancer, and the doctors give him three to six months to live."

A dead quiet came over the room. Not a word was spoken for the longest time. Finally, my mother explained everything, but once I heard that Dad only had a few months left to live, I shut down. I saw Mom's lips moving, but I couldn't hear what she was saying. I just stared at her as if she were lying to us. I was praying that she was lying. This could not be true.

How is it possible that my father is going to die?

Before now, I only remembered one death in the family. That was when I was fifteen, visiting my brother and sister-in-law out of town. We got a call from my mother that my grandfather on Dad's side had died. He was my favorite relative; Grandpa Ed was my buddy. Because I was out of town, my parents wouldn't let me fly to Los Angeles for his funeral. I was very upset.

Now, I could not lose my dad, my hero, the one I went to about anything. I could talk to him and know that I wouldn't be judged. He would present the options that I couldn't see.

This intelligent, good, honest man can't die! What will I do without my daddy?

"Judy... Judy?" my mother asked. "Did you understand everything? Do you have any questions?"

I finally snapped back to the present.

"Yeah, Mom. I got it. So, is there any chance that he could live longer?"

"No, Judy. He is terminal. We're going to have to come up with a plan to take care of him as long as possible here at home. That way, he'll feel more comfortable, and we can all be with him."

"Is he going to be able to come home for Christmas?" I asked Mom.

"I don't know. We'll cross that bridge when it gets here. Right now, I need to make some arrangements for a hospital bed to be delivered, and a few other things he'll need once he does come home."

"Mom, do you need me for anything right now? Can I take Dad's car and go for a short ride? I need to let this all sink in."

"Sure, you can. Don't be gone too long, however. I'll want you here this afternoon to help with some things."

"Okay. I'll be back."

I got Dad's car keys out of the wooden bowl they kept on the desk in the corner of the dining room. Grabbed my purse and was out the garage door. Into Dad's blue Ford Maverick, backing out of the garage and onto the street. I took off and headed for Cherry Lane. It was a road that went up into the eastside foothills of town. It was a good five-mile, two-lane drive out through the horse fields, cow pastures, and pear orchards. Not too many homes up here yet, but give them twenty years and it would be packed with housing. What a shame this beautiful, serene drive would someday be no more.

For now, though, it was my solitude. My space. I could drive around the hill, smoke a joint, and try to wrap my head around my father's situation.

I can't lose him! I can't talk to Mom the way I can talk to Dad. She doesn't understand me, whereas Dad does. He gets the fact that I am my own person now and can make my own decisions. For God's sake, I'm 28, Mom. I'm an adult.

I have walked out of my own wedding. That was a major decision in my life. I decided to leave Oregon to move to Los Angeles to return to school. I couldn't be myself with Mom for fear she would judge me. Dad never judged; he weighed the issues before rendering his opinion. That was the attorney in him.

My mind was racing everywhere. I just could not believe that I was about to lose my father.

This isn't fair. He still has to walk me down the aisle when I do find Mr. Right.

I was gone quite some time, and thought it best to head back. I pulled into the garage at home, closing the garage door behind me. I walked into the dining room. Mom and Hat were there.

"I spoke to the doctor," Mom said, "and he said that your father can come home on Christmas day, but then he has to go back until he is well enough to come home. I ordered a hospital bed, but it won't be delivered for a week. That should be about the time they let him out."

"That's good. It wouldn't be Christmas without him," I said, realizing that this will be my last Christmas with my dad.

Christmas morning rolled around and my brother went to the hospital to bring Dad home. Richard helped him into the house. Dad wanted to sit in the living room next to the Christmas tree. He was wearing his white terry cloth robe over his navy-blue pajamas, with white socks and brown house slippers. Dad was not looking very good. His cheeks were starting to sink in, and he was obviously losing weight. His skin had a slight tinge of yellow because his kidneys were slowly starting to malfunction.

We tried to have a "normal" Christmas. No one mentioned the fact that we all knew this is Dad's last Christmas with us. It was bittersweet that we had him with us now. Mom and Hat took pictures of us, and I specifically remembered this one picture taken of Dad by himself on the couch. He already looked half dead. I didn't like all the pictures that were being taken because I knew they would be his last.

I don't want to lose my dad!

We ate dinner early, around 2:30 in the afternoon. Dad was getting tired and was ready to go back to the hospital for the night. We all wished him a Merry Christmas and gave him our love and hugs, then Richard took him back to his hospital room.

It was a very quiet night around the house. It was as if no one wanted to talk about the situation because that would make it more real. After Mom and Hat finished their bourbon and waters, they joined me in the dining/family room to watch television.

"Watch what you want," I said. "I'm going into your bedroom to call my girlfriend."

I talked with her for about a half hour. It was still early, but I wanted to be alone, so I went out to the other room to say my good nights, and off to my room I went.

Was lying on my bed, thinking it was just a month ago that I almost died in the fire. Now I was finding out that my dad only had months to live.

How cruel can life be? Sadly, I would get an answer in two months' time. Always be careful of what you ask the universe. It is capable of coming back with some heavy-duty answers that you may not like. And never say "worse," because it can always get worse.

The next morning, I slept in until about nine o'clock. I got up, went to the kitchen, and poured myself a bowl of Cheerios. Mom and Hat were already on their third cups of coffee for the morning.

Mom said to me, "We have been talking about how we can keep your father at home for as long as possible. You're not working right now, are you?"

"No, Mom, I'm not. And even if my boss had more work for me, she would totally understand that I have to be here with my family. So don't worry about it."

"Well, okay, but since you're not working, I want to pay your bills for the month."

"That's not necessary, Mom. Thank you, I appreciate the offer, but I'm okay right now."

"Harriet and I have been talking, and if you could arrange to be up here when the time comes that your father will need round-the-clock attention, would you be willing to be the one that sits up with him at night, and Hat and I will take care of him during the day?"

"Certainly, Mom. I would be happy to take care of him at night. I've got some beading projects I want to work on, and that would be a good time to work on them after the TV goes off for the night. You know I'm a night person, so it's no problem. Just give me a little notice so I can find a cat sitter and I will be right up."

That afternoon, we all went up to the hospital to visit Dad. Along with us was Richard's fourteen-year-old son, Paul. Mom and Hat were on the right side of Dad's bed, while Paul was at the foot, with Richard and me on Dad's left. He was talking to each of us, one-on-one. When he got to my brother, Dad said, "Richard, now you be sure to take care of your little sister."

Richard just nodded. He and I weren't exactly each other's fans. In fact, he had hated me from the day they brought me home. First of all, he was no longer the "Miracle Child." It took Mom and Dad six years before they got pregnant with him. They were both told they could never have children. Needless to say, my big brother was spoiled rotten.

Secondly, I was a girl, therefore I was instantly "Daddy's Little Girl." My brother did not like the competition. It only got worse as we matured; you will hear about this at a later date.

My brother is a true ass, at least to me and his two ex-wives. But I'm getting ahead of myself. Sit tight… you won't miss a thing.

The week passed very quickly. Richard had returned home to Albany, a couple hours north. That next Monday, the hospital bed was delivered and set up in Mom and Dad's bedroom. Mom moved their two single beds out so we could fit the dark green leather couch from the family room in there, as well. It was basically set up as Dad's own private hospital room. We had the small television in there so either he or whoever was with him could watch it. Dad came home that night. It was really great to have him home again.

I was home for another three days before I had to fly back to Los Angeles. Dad and I had some good talks about when I was growing up. We reminisced about many things. One time we talked about the time that I went to pick him up at the Portland airport when I was living there and he was flying in for a work meeting. We got in my 1973 Mustang, which had baby blue paint with a white vinyl top. She was my baby.

As I drove away from the airport Dad asked,

"Where is your ashtray?" He was going to have a cigarette.

"Oh, it's right here, Dad." I pulled open the ashtray between the bucket seats, and laying in there was a roach clip with a roach on it. A quiet chill came over me.

I'm dead now.

Dad simply said, "I think it's time you cleaned out your car."

"Yes, Dad. I've been meaning to do that. I'll take care of it as soon as I get home."

The funny thing was, he never said a word about me smoking marijuana to my mother. She would have totally freaked. Dad, on the other hand, had openly said that he thought marijuana should be legalized and taxed the hell out of. My father was somewhat of a visionary.

We had a fabulous time talking about things we had experienced together, including our fishing trips. Only he and I would go fishing; my brother was never interested. Dad and I had some good talks out on the river. He also taught me how to play golf. Everyone in my family played golf. My brother always played when Dad and I went fishing.

To this day, I am so glad I had those extra couple of days to spend with him before I went back home to LA. By the end of January, my mother called me. "Judy, I think it's time for you to pack and get back up here. Your dad is not doing too well and does need someone to sit with him at night now. He sleeps most of the time, but when he's awake, you need to help him.

I've bought a plane ticket for you. I hope the day after tomorrow isn't too soon?"

"No, Mom, that will be fine. I just have to do some laundry and throw some things in a suitcase, and I'm ready to go. What time on Monday do I leave?"

"You fly out of LAX at noon and arrive in Medford about four. I'll be there to pick you up."

"Okay, Mom. Just park out front of the airport. I'll find you once I get my bag. That way, you won't have to park and come in."

"That sounds fine, dear. Thank you very much. I'll see you Monday afternoon. I love you."

"I love you, too, Mom. Give Dad my love with a kiss and a hug. Tell him I'll see him in a couple of days."

"Oh, he knows and he is already looking forward to seeing you. You take care now. Goodbye."

"Goodbye, Mom."

A couple days later, I was at home in Medford. Mom picked me up from the airport and we headed straight to the house. After I unloaded my bags, I took them into the house and put them in the den. I went back out to the kitchen. Harriet wasn't there at the moment.

I turned to Mom and said, "I brought up some joints that I'm going to put in Dad's nightstand drawer. If he wants to smoke them, please don't give him a bad time about it. It will give him an appetite and help with the pain."

Mom looked at me like I had spoken a foreign language.

"What are you talking about?" she asked with a very questioning look on her face.

Oh shhhhhit! Dad never told her I smoke pot! Fuck! I just busted myself to my own mother. Well, this is going to be an interesting time at home.

"Mom, I brought Dad some marijuana cigarettes. If he wants to smoke one, please don't give him a hard time. We have talked about his feelings about marijuana and he is fine with it."

"Are you saying that you smoke marijuana? Since when? Moving to Hollywood, I bet. I knew that place was nothing but sex and drugs."

"Don't forget the Rock & Roll! Seriously, Mom, you know no such thing. There are normal people that live very normal lives in LA. You're just talking about what you read on the cover of the *Enquirer.*"

"No, I'm not. I have friends and I hear what goes on down there."

"Please, let's just drop the subject. This is about Dad, anyway, not me."

I headed back to my suitcase in the den and took out three joints. I took them into Dad's room. He was sleeping at the moment, so I very quietly placed the joints in the drawer next to his bed.

Dad was not looking good at all. Jaundice had set in real good by now. His skin and eyes were yellowish and his cheeks were very sunken. He was just skin and bone, practically. He spent all his time in bed now, unable to get into the wheelchair and roll around the house. It was a good thing they moved in the leather couch; we could all be in there at once if we wanted.

The way Mom and Harriet worked it out was that Mom would be up first with Dad, fix his breakfast and be his main caregiver until about mid-afternoon, when Hat would take over. She would care for him until about ten at night. Then I would get up, have my breakfast, which was usually leftover dinner, and that was fine with me. I'd have a sandwich, or something halfway through the night, and my Cheerios when it was time to go to bed at about six or seven in the morning. I slept on the couch in the living room every day. I could sleep anywhere, and the couch was very comfortable. That way, Mom or Hat could use the other bedroom to lay down with the door closed if they wanted to.

At night, when I was up with Dad, we were no longer able to have our long talks. He wore out very quickly, which was understandable, with the heavy-duty meds the doctors had him on. He did sleep most of the night, but would wake up every few hours and want a sip of water or an ice cube to suck on. I would get the glass and guide the straw to his lips, as he would then hold the straw with his long, thin fingers that were nothing but knuckles now.

I would also have to hold the drip pan under his chin for any spillage, then very gently wipe the corners of his mouth. Dad would look at me and not have to say a word.

"I know, Dad. I love you, too!"

He would be awake for maybe five, ten minutes at the longest, and I would sit next to him, holding his hand. Then, off he would drift into who knows where and fall fast asleep again. Dad wasn't in a coma or anything, but I often wondered if he could still see and hear what was going on around him when he was asleep.

The master bath was right there, a few feet from Dad's bed. I would go in there after Johnny Carson was over, pull out my little mirror, razor, and short straw. Yes, I did coke after the television stations turned off for the night.

I must admit, a time or two, I felt very guilty because it was like Dad was watching me, hovering over me and witnessing my behavior. The last thing I wanted was for him to know that his "Little Girl" did blow. And God forbid... if my mother were to ever find out. *Lord, help me.*

See, this was the reason Mom and I couldn't talk to each other in depth. She was very Catholic, and I was very Hollywood now. I didn't do that much coke, except after Dad died. Then I did have a slight issue for only a couple of months. Once I realized that— instead of spending $300 on a gram of coke, I could buy a fabulous pair of Italian designer, high heels—my shoe addiction began and my coke habit ended, which was really only about a gram a week. I stretched it out as far as I could.

Hell, I watched musicians snort a half gram in one line. Geez, that would kill me! Besides, I saw it as "what a waste." I wanted to stretch it out. But then, when you have all the money you could ever want, what's a little heavier coke habit? No, thank you, not for me. But I must admit, when I did get my coke, it was from the musician who supplied the big-name artists. It was extremely good coke.

After my trip to the bathroom, I would sit on the green leather couch and work on my beading project. I wanted to make a black silk satin Cowgirl shirt with beaded fringe that had a rose pattern in the beads. I had no idea what I had gotten myself into with that project. At least it kept me busy. I never did finish enough fringe to make the blouse. It was 1980, the year that the movie *Urban Cowboy* with John Travolta was released.

As frail as Dad was getting, he was still very much aware mentally. In the strangest way, time seemed to go so very slow, yet overall, it passed more quickly than I would have wanted it to. With each week, Dad would lose just a little more of himself, either in terms of weight or the whites of his eyes. By week three in February, they were very yellow.

I remember the weekend of the 21st. Odd I would have these feelings on this day. It was now exactly three months since the MGM fire. I couldn't shake the feeling that Dad was dying. I couldn't help it; I saw it in his face every day. I just wanted his pain to end, but I didn't want him to leave me. What was I going to do without my dad? He had always been there.

Mom was sitting in the kitchen when I approached her and said,

"Mom, Dad is dying and I need a break. I gotta get out of here for a few days. Can I take his car and drive down to LA, pay my bills, see the cat, and I will be right back? I'll only be gone two days."

"I know you need a break. This is not easy for any of us. We'll have to talk to your father and see what he says."

"Okay. That sounds good. I definitely want him to know that I will be right back in two days. I won't be gone that long."

When Dad was awake for lunch, both Mom and I went into his room.

Mom said, "Wally, Judy needs to go down to LA for a couple of days to pay her bills. We were thinking she could take your car since she flew up."

Dad took my hand and said, "You need to take care of that. Yes, take the Maverick and be careful. But I know you will be;

you're a very good driver. Just stay off the gas." He cracked a little smile."Yes, Dad. I will watch my speed. I'll be very careful. I was looking at the weather, and it's going to be foggy for a few days, but Tuesday, it looks like there will be a break. So, I'll still be here with you at night for a few more days. This is only Saturday."

"Good," he said. "I like having you nearby. I'm feeling a little tired now. I think I'll take my afternoon nap. I love you both."

"I love you, too, Dad."

"Love you, Wally."

We left his room. The next few nights were the roughest. He had a couple of bad nights where the pain was so bad, it was hard for him to sleep. When he would sleep, he would be twitching from the pain. I felt so helpless. I just wanted to make him better.

Tuesday the 24th finally rolled around. I threw just a few things in my suitcase for myself, knowing I was doing a turn and burn. I had laid down about five o'clock and slept until ten. When I got up, it was still a little foggy out. I wanted to jump in the car and leave, but Mom insisted that I wait just a little while longer.

Finally, by eleven, the grayish, cold fog was lifting. I went into Dad's room to let him know I was heading out.

"Hey, Dad. The fog is lifting, so I'm going to go ahead and take off now."

"You be very careful and I'll see you in two days. Now if you get tired, you pull over, understand?"

"Yes, Dad. I'll be fine. You take care of yourself, and don't give Mom and Hat too much of a hard time. I love you very much." And I leaned over to kiss him goodbye.

"Goodbye, Toots." That was his nickname for me.

I walked out of the bedroom, stopping at the door to blow him a kiss and a smile. I turned and walked down the long hallway to the entryway. I stopped at the corner, turning around to see Dad in the full-length mirror hanging on the door one more time, laying in that hospital bed. He looked so small and frail. A tear started to form in my right eye, as I quickly wiped it away. I didn't want Mom to see me cry. I knew in my heart this was the last time I would see my father alive.

I walked up to Mom in the kitchen and said, "I'll call you at six o'clock, no matter where I am. I do plan to drive straight through, though. But I'll talk to you at six. I love you, Mom." I gave her a big hug.

"All right," Mom said. "I'll be looking forward to the call. You be careful now."

"I will. Now stop worrying. Bye."

I walked out the garage door to the driveway, where I had warmed up the car. I put my suitcase in the trunk, closed it, and by this time, Mom had made it out to the car for one final goodbye.

I hugged her, gave her a kiss, and got in the car. Then I removed my cowboy boots and put on my fuzzy booties. I was more comfortable driving that way. I pulled down the street, turning the corner, and pulled over to the curb. I needed to get my pipe and bag of weed out of my purse. I loaded the pipe, had my lighter handy, and I was now truly ready to get on the road.

I hit the freeway by about 11:20 and was on my way home to LA. I hated to leave Dad, but I had to get out of there. I just couldn't take watching him slowly dying before my eyes. It was just too painful.

The weather wasn't too bad. The fog had lifted, but going up the north side of the Siskiyou Summit, I did hit fog again. As soon as I crossed over the Oregon/California border, the fog was gone.

Just clear road and cloudy skies. About five miles south of the border was an agricultural stop. The California Highway Patrol officers were inevitably always there. Needless to say, I had not started smoking anything yet.

As always, they were stopping all the cars headed south. I rolled up to the little station, where they asked,

"Where are you coming from? Do you have any fresh fruit with you?"

"No, sir, and I just left Medford."

"Have a safe trip."

"Thank you." I drove off to re-enter the freeway, where the CHP usually sat. I waited until I was a good five miles down the road, making sure that none of the CHP pulled out onto the interstate before I lit my pipe. The music of our local radio station was cranked up loud. Only problem was that I lost the reception about ten miles up the mountain.

An hour into the drive, I had smoked several bowls of pot and managed to down a Dr. Pepper.

Not only did I lose my grandfather, now I'm losing my dad, and to the best of my knowledge, I have already lost Tom. They are the three most important men in my life, now I have none of them.

A tear started rolling down my left cheek, and before I knew it, I was in a full-blown cry. After about five minutes, I realized I needed to pull myself together. I thought I saw a snowflake or two flying by.

A couple miles down I-5 southbound, I spotted a sign for a rest area. Fabulous! My eyeballs were floating and I desperately needed to pee. By the time I got to the rest area and pulled over to park, the snow was coming down a little quicker. I first put on my boots, then struggled to get my zip-up hoodie on, pulling the hoodie over my hair. In the numbing cold, I dashed to the ladies room. The toilet seat, even with the seat gasket on, was extremely chilly. I was in and out as quickly as possible.

Back at the car, I took off my zip-up, tossing it to the passenger's seat. Preoccupied by the amount of snow that was coming down now, I totally spaced on taking off my cowboy boots. I backed the car up, then headed out to the freeway again. The snow was starting to stick to the road. I was not too concerned at the moment. As I was crossing a bridge at Lakehead, a small town on Lake Shasta in northern California, I made the sign of the cross.

"Jesus and Angel Bob, please get me to Redding safely!"

It was only about twenty-five minutes away, but driving through the mountains with the snow coming down at an alarmingly fast rate was not my idea of a good time.

I took a deep breath and prayed for the best. I could no longer see the road. The snow was about two inches thick and the snowflakes were the size of silver dollars. I was following in the tire tracks of the car in front of me. That was the only way I could tell I was still on the road and in a lane. There was not much traffic. We came to a bend in the road as it curved to the right around a mountain. I was realizing that I had little traction and it was very slippery outside.

All of a sudden, I looked up at the top of the mountain and a semi-truck was coming around the northbound curve rather quickly. Then everything moved in slow motion.

The truck jackknifed.

It was heading towards me.

My mind flashes with options to react and avoid disaster.

I can't look away from the truck's flatbed falling onto its side, careening straight at me.

I had no traction, so swerving to get out of his way was not an option. In fact, I had no options. I was going to die. So, with the flatbed just yards from my car, I let go of the wheel and lay down on the bench seat in the Maverick.

The flatbed hitting the car made loud, mashing metal noises. It rolled over the Maverick, making everything pitch black for a moment, with more harsh rumbling sounds. Then, absolute silence as I laid on the seat.

Am I dead?

The car was completely smashed in on the driver's side. I would soon learn that had the truck hit a foot differently either way, its load would have smashed the entire car.

When all was said and done, the car had never left the ground. It was sitting on all four tires, facing the snowy mountain.

And I just laid there.

Am I alive or dead?

I sat up. Bright white snow was everywhere.

Oh, my God! I must be dead.

A warm trickle of blood was running down the right side of my face. *If I'm bleeding… I must be alive.*

Then, like a lightning bolt, it hit me: *Get the hell out of this car!* That was around the time that the Ford Pinto's were catching on fire and blowing up. This was a Maverick, just a glorified Pinto, which I believed was going to blow any moment.

I first tried to get out of the driver's side, then realized there was no driver's side. So I scooted up to the passenger door, trying to open it. Unfortunately, it was jammed shut. I pounded my right shoulder into it a couple of times, but that did not work.

My cowboy boots! I was still wearing them. So I laid back, facing the passenger door, and kicked the door as hard as I could. Nothing.

Panic set in. I didn't want to go up in flames in this car. I laid back again with another swift kick to the door. Nothing. Finally, I kicked one more time, with all my might.

And it opened.

I shot up and out of that car! As I ran away from it, the trucker who had jackknifed came running towards me shouting, "Are you okay? Are you okay?"

"I think I am. I don't feel anything broken," I said, with blood gushing out of my head, down my face, and onto my favorite shirt. It was a purple sweatshirt fabric with a graphic square block print on the back. You had to look at it long enough to read that it said, "Fuck Off."

What a delightful shirt to be stuck in for all the world to see.

The trucker said, "You need to lay back down in your car in case you have a concussion. Plus, you're bleeding like a stuck pig."

"I am not getting back in that car. It's going to catch fire and blow up! And I want no part of that."

"Look, ma'am. You're hurt! You need to lay down. At least until the ambulance gets here."

"What part of NO don't you understand?" I shouted, probably going into shock. "I'm not getting back in that car!"

A hippie chick who was about my age, mid-20s or so, approached, assuring me that it was perfectly safe to lay down in the car. Her voice was very soothing and peaceful.

An uncanny, weird calmness came over me. I walked with her as she led me back to my car. The passenger door was still open and she had me sit on the edge of the seat.

She asked, "Is there anything I can do for you?"

"Yes! Would you please try to find my pipe and the bag of weed I have in the front seat and put them in my suitcase in the trunk?"

It seemed as if she found both in no time at all. Next, she said, "I got them both and they are safely tucked away in the zipper of your suitcase."

"Thank you so much. You have no idea how much that means to me."

Next thing I know, there is a nun asking of my condition and if there was anything she could do to help.

"No, thank you. I am fine, and this very nice gal has already helped me."

The nun replied, "Who did you say helped you? Because I don't see anyone."

"She's right there to your left. She's the hippie chick."

"No, there's no one here but us."

Okay, if there is no one there, then who just helped me? I know I got hit in the head, but I'm not delusional.

I did see her. She found my pot and put it in the trunk. I heard the trunk lid close. So where did she go? One minute she was there, talking so calming to me, and the next she was gone? I just sat there wondering if Angel Bob had anything to do with her help.

Next thing I knew, the nun was handing me a small clean towel to put on my head, in hopes of stopping the bleeding. The blood had dripped all down the front of my favorite shirt.

Shit… blood stains are the worst to get out.

The nun said, "They have ambulances coming. I'll go check with them and inform them that you have a head wound." And off she went.

I was now sitting on the edge of the seat with my feet out the door.

If I'm going to sit here, I'm going to be able to get out quickly if need be. There was no way I was going to lay down in the seat. I sat there for what seemed like forever. Just my luck, my Dr. Pepper was going through me. I could pee anytime. Not drastically yet, but enough for my brain to bring it to my attention. Gee, thanks.

A fireman finally came around to check me out.

"It might be a bit longer before we can get to you," he said, somewhat apologetically. "The car in front of you was hit pretty hard, and we have four badly injured passengers to get on their way to the hospital first. So, sit tight and we'll get to you as soon as we can."

"Thank you, sir. I certainly appreciate your help."

It must have been a good twenty to thirty minutes before the medics were ready to take a look at me.

"Are you feeling any pain?" they asked.

"Yes, I have a hell of a headache, and my neck hurts."

They looked at my wound, cleaned it up and tried to stop the bleeding. "You should be fine," they said. "It looks like a small surface wound."

They checked me out completely to make sure nothing was broken. They were mostly concerned about a concussion. They kept talking to me so I wouldn't fall asleep.

"I have to go to the bathroom," I told one of them. "Will it be much longer?"

The medic said, "It's a good twenty-minute drive into Redding to Mercy Medical Center. We can always put in a catheter."

"Oh, no, thank you. I'll just hold it."

We arrived at the hospital after what seemed like hours to get there. They wheeled me into the emergency room, finding an open spot for my gurney. The nurses immediately surrounded me, checking me and hooking me up to machines. Apparently, all my vitals were good.

"Excuse me," I said, "but I really need to use the restroom. Where is it?"

One of the passing nurses replied, "Oh, you can't move until we get an x-ray of your neck and back. It shouldn't be too much longer."

I had to pee so badly, I thought I was going to explode! After what felt like an eternity, they finally wheeled me down to x-ray, took the films, then returned me to my little spot in the ER. The nurse finally let me use the restroom. When I sat down and I released my bladder, I thought it would never stop. Finally, relief! I washed up and returned to my gurney.

Then in came the ER doctor to stitch up the wound on my head.

Nervously, I asked, "Is it absolutely necessary for you to stitch it?"

They had me sit up straight on the gurney and clean out the inch-long cut. Mavericks did not have gloveboxes; they had a shelf under the dash. My father kept a glass ashtray on that shelf for his cigarettes while he was driving. That ashtray had a couple of glass handles, about an inch long. Apparently that hit me in the head to cause the gash.

By the time the doctor was finished with my five stitches, I was practically laying on the gurney. I would scoot down every time he put a stitch in my head. It was not a pleasant experience.

They gave me a neck brace to wear for at least a week and advised me to see my own doctor when I got home. They were all finished with me, and gave me a small bottle of pain pills to take for the headache and the sore muscles I was going to inevitably experience in the next couple of days.

"You're free to go," they said.

My question was, "Go where?"

I had no car. I just had my purse—not even my hoodie to protect from the cold weather. I had no choice. I went to a payphone in the hospital and called a taxi. When they arrived to collect me, the only place I could think to go was the Holiday Inn at the freeway. He dropped me at the front door. I paid him and exited the taxi.

I went up to the front desk and informed the clerk that I had just been in an accident and I needed a room for the night. While handing him my credit card, I noticed a clock on the wall. It said 5:40.

Shit! I have to call Mom at six o'clock. I told her I would, no matter where I was. By the time the clerk finished checking me in and I got to my room, it was ten minutes to six.

At the hospital, they had given me some Valium. I took one, chewing it so it would take effect faster. I also found a glass for a drink of water. This was the worst phone call I ever had to make. I thought calling Mom about the MGM fire was bad enough. But now, she not only had a husband of forty years on his deathbed, but her daughter has been in a horrible car accident. How was I going to tell her this?

At six o'clock on the dot, I picked up the telephone receiver and dialed her number.

Mom answered, "Hello."

"I'm okay, but I killed Dad's car."

That was all that I could get out. "But I'm okay, I promise."

I burst into tears, crying uncontrollably.

"What happened? Are you sure you're all right?"

"There was this snowstorm that came out of nowhere. This semi-truck jackknifed going north around a corner at the top of the hill, speeding, of course, and he ran over another car, then me, and landed with his cab of the truck dangling over a car with a couple from Canada in it."

How ironic that there was a Canadian couple at the MGM, and now another one. Was this some strange coincidence or what?

I told her, "It's still snowing here. I don't know how I'm going to get home."

"I'll send your brother down to get you. But we'll have to wait until this storm passes."

"Okay, Mom. Will we be able to find where they took the car? My suitcase is still in the trunk with all my things."

"Don't you worry about that. I'll make some phone calls and find out where the car is. We'll need to, anyway, for the insurance. You just get some rest and don't worry about anything."

"How is Dad doing?"

"He's doing just fine. I'll give him your love. You take care now, and I'll call you when I know Richard will be coming down to get you."

"Okay. Thanks, Mom. I'm so sorry I am putting you through all of this. It's all my fault. I should have never left to go to LA."

"Now just stop that. It is what it is, and we will get through this. You get some rest and I will talk to you tomorrow. I love you. Goodbye."

"I love you, too, Mom. Goodbye."

I hung up and laid on the bed.

I was completely lost. I really wanted to smoke something but, unfortunately, I had nothing. It was all in the trunk of the car. Thank God. At least they gave me a few pain pills and some Valium. I would need it to help me sleep tonight.

Restless, I paced the room, my mind racing with everything.

Dad dying, me wrecking his car, this snowstorm, Mom going through all this without me there with her. My mind wouldn't stop. I finally took a Valium, hoping to calm the heck down.

I found the television remote control and turned it on. I went to the bathroom, taking off my jeans so I could crawl into bed. I had no toothbrush, so I substituted a washcloth by rubbing it across my teeth until they felt somewhat cleaner. I figured that was better than nothing.

Looking in the mirror, I hardly recognized myself. For starters, I was a mess. My hair was all over the place. Thank goodness I had my brush in my purse with a hair tie wrapped around it for emergencies. *I think this constitutes an emergency.*

Damn, Judy, what the fuck! I can't believe what has just happened. I can't believe the car was so mashed in on the driver's side that I walked away from that accident.

When the flatbed of the semi slammed into my car, it totally smashed in the driver's roof and door. There was basically nothing left of the driver's side. Staring at myself, I was in shock. Dried blood caked around my hairline. The ER doctor had to shave just a little spot so he could stitch me up.

I went back to the bed, fluffing up the pillows so I could sit up. As I laid on the bed, I kept playing the accident over and over in my mind— seeing the flatbed coming down the hill, dragging the cab of the truck with it as it barreled ever closer to me. All in slow motion.

I couldn't really say that my life flashed before my eyes. It was more like time had slowed down to a crawl, giving me enough time to let go of the wheel and lay down on the front seat. If I had not done that, I wouldn't be here, and the sheriff would have been the one calling Mom.

Angel Bob, I have no one to thank but you and God!

My jaw is screwed up and I have five stitches in my head. I would say, for just being run over by a semi-truck, I was actually doing quite well. I was one extremely lucky lady.

Bob, I can't thank you enough for getting me through that mess. I thought being hit by a train was jolting, but this was much worse. I honestly thought I was dead. Thank you, thank you, thank you, Bob!

I woke up the next morning with quite the headache, but worse was how sore my entire body was from the jolt of the hit. I sat up on the side of the bed, putting both my hands on either side of me on the mattress, hanging my head down, just emotionally numb. Damn, I was sore from my neck to my feet. To avoid the obvious, I felt like I had just been run over by a semi-truck. And I had.

I stood up very slowly to walk to the bathroom. Boy, this was one morning I really wished I had something to smoke. In the bathroom, I got myself a glass of water. It was definitely time for one of the pain pills the doctor gave me. I put on my pants and shoes to go down the hall to the vending machines for a cold soda. Unfortunately, they had Coke, no Pepsi. However, there was a nice cold can of Dr. Pepper with my name on it. *That should help wake me up.*

Back in the room, I was getting immensely anxious. I went to the nightstand by the bed and took one of the Valium pills from the hospital. Pacing the room again, carrying the can of soda, my mind raced once again. I was thinking of my mother and how she must have been handling all that was happening. I decided to call my Aunt Gen, my mother's sister, hoping that she would fly out to be with Mom.

"Hello, Aunt Gen. This is your niece, Judy." She also had a daughter named Judy. "Well, hello, Judy. How are you doing?"

"I'm not doing well. I left Mom and Dad's yesterday to go home to Los Angeles and pay my bills, but I didn't make it out of the mountains. I was run over by a semi-truck."

"What? My God, are you okay?"

"Yes, fortunately. I had five stitches in my head and it screwed up my jaw. They said my TMJ was dislocated. I'll need to see my dentist when I get back to Medford."

"Where are you now?"

"I'm at a Holiday Inn in Redding. The snowstorm that came through, that caused all of this, is supposed to stop by tonight. I'm hoping that Richard can come down and get me. The reason I'm calling is to ask you if you could fly out to be with Mom while she's going through Dad's dying and my accident?"

"Judy, I just can't make it out there right now," Aunt Gen said. "I'm sorry, but it's just not possible."

I practically begged her to come out. I got very emotional and was in tears about everything. You could say I was a little hysterical. But Gen reassured me that everything would be fine and that Mom and I would get through this together.

It wasn't until a few years later that I learned the real reason Gen would not come out to Oregon. Apparently, Gen was still upset with my mother when she wouldn't, or couldn't, go be with Gen when her husband passed away. So, I guess there was a little payback involved.

I never really knew much about my mother. She never talked about herself and her life up until she married Dad. After Mom's death, I tried to get some information out of Aunt Gen, but she was tight-lipped, too. I guess it was their generation. You didn't talk about your issues; you just dealt with them.

After we got off the phone, I was going crazy. I felt like a trapped animal that couldn't escape a cage. The snow was still coming down, but not as hard as the day before. It did seem that the storm was passing.

But with each passing moment, I was going nuts. I took more drugs. I spread them out, so I wouldn't run out of anything before I got back to Medford to see Mom's doctor. Why didn't I have that hippie chick put my pot in my purse? Because I didn't want to get caught with it. After all, it was still illegal then.

I didn't want anyone to see me in this state, so I ordered room service for lunch. I had a club sandwich, thinking it would last me through dinner. Mom and I spoke late that morning.

"How are you feeling, Judy?"

"I'm extremely sore. My whole body hurts. How is Dad doing?"

"He's hanging in there. Your brother will be heading out in the morning, about eight or nine, whenever the weather is safe over the pass. He should be there between noon and one."

"Okay, Mom. I'll be here. I don't have much else to do."

"All right, Judy, you take care, and I'll see you tomorrow. Goodbye."

"Give Dad a hug and kiss for me. I'll talk to you later. Bye." And I hang up the phone.

Well, one more day to go stir-crazy in this motel room. I couldn't handle it much longer. I was pacing the room again.

This is nuts! I need to settle down. There is nothing I can do for Dad from here. I need to be patient until Richard can pick me up.

I sat on the bed with my feet up. I wanted to call my girlfriend, Pamela, but I knew she was still sleeping. I had to wait until noon before I bothered her. I found something on TV to watch, but my mind was on Dad and how he was doing.

Finally, it was noon. I reached for the phone, dialing Pamela's number. It rang several times before she picked up. "Hi, Pamela.

It's me. So, what was the name of that shrink you wanted me to see? I think I need him now."

"Are you okay? What has changed? Did your father die?"

"No, Dad hasn't died yet. But I am not doing too well. I'm stuck in Redding waiting for my brother to come get me."

"What are you doing in Redding?"

"I was headed to LA when I was run over by a semi-truck."

I went through the whole story with her and brought her up to date about how I was doing all alone in the hotel room. Around one o'clock, I looked out the window and the snow had stopped.

"I better get going," I said. "This is going to be one expensive phone call. I'll give you a call in a few days and let you know what's going on and when I will be home."

"Okay, Judy. You take care of yourself. I'm worried about you."

"Don't be. I'll be fine. I just need to get home. Take care. Bye."

We hung up. I felt a little better, but not much. I was all talked out by this time.

The second Valium must be kicking in, as I'm starting to feel tired.

I drift off to sleep, which was the best thing for me at the moment.

I woke a few hours later, my body feeling the pain again. Slowly rolling over and into a sitting-up position, I just sat there for a few moments, collecting myself, realizing it was later than I thought.

No wonder I'm hungry, it's almost five. I better call for room service again. I can't live on vending machine food. Besides, I'm running out of cash. This way, I can charge it to the room.

I ordered up a hamburger this time, with a pickle on the side.

About half an hour later, room service knocked on my door with the food. The young man brought in the tray. I tipped him a dollar on his way out. I took the tray over to the bed so I could be comfortable while eating. The burger was fat and juicy, with just the right amount of tomato, onion, and lettuce. No mayo! I ate about half of it and saved the other half for later. The side dish of potato salad was actually pretty good, with the right amount of tang; I ate it all.

The evening news was on with the weather report. The storm had blown out of the area and we were looking at clear skies for a couple of days. Fabulous! Richard could leave early in the morning and I would be out of here by noon. I fell asleep to some show that was on after the news and slept until about two in the morning.

I woke up, wide awake, with no idea why. I went to the bathroom, washed up, and returned to bed, where I finished the hamburger. Wasn't too bad cold.

Fortunately, the Holiday Inn had HBO, so after the regular stations went off the air, I still had something to watch. I was awake through almost a full movie, and of course, fell asleep just as they were ready to reveal who the real killer was. Needless to say, by the time I woke up again, it was a moot point.

My phone rang at about eight. I was still in that half-asleep, half-awake mode. I jumped to attention and grabbed the phone.

"Hello."

"Good morning, Judy. I wanted to let you know that your brother is on his way. He just left and should be there in about two or three hours."

"Okay, Mom, thank you. I'll be ready. It's not like I have any luggage or anything. I'll see you and Dad later this afternoon."

"Yes, I look forward to seeing you. I want to make sure you're all right. You take care, goodbye."

"Goodbye, Mom, I love you." She just hung up and most likely did not hear *the* "I *love you*" part.

It was tough, the "I love you" part. I noticed a couple years ago, we never said it to each other. It was just something that was understood. As I grew older, I started to realize how important it is to hear someone say to you that they love you. It was surprisingly tough for me to say at the end of a phone conversation, but I would force myself to say it. Eventually, it caught on, and Mom started to say it back to me. This took quite some time for her to say it. She was from that generation where you didn't say that stuff. You just knew.

After about six months, I noticed it was easy for her to say it to me now. Of course, Dad got in on it, too. Before long, we were using it regularly. It was reassuring to hear and nice to know that they were conveying feelings that they didn't talk about even ten years ago.

However, Mother wasn't completely upfront with me about Dad's condition. She somewhat neglected to tell me that Dad was taken back to the hospital on Wednesday. She didn't want me to freak out because I wasn't there. I wouldn't have been able to do anything, but I certainly could have been with my father.

I gathered up my belongings and fit everything into my purse. That was all I have with me. It would feel so good to get out of these dirty, bloody clothes and into some fresh, clean things.

After pacing for about an hour, I sat on the bed. More anxious than ever, I wanted to go home and see my dad! The waiting was unbearable. So I dove into my purse, in search of Valium. Upon finding the bottle, I opened it and took one more. I only had a couple left. I called Mom back and she answered. "Hello."

"Hi, Mom, it's just me. Would you do me a favor, please? Would you call your doctor and see if I can get in to be checked out? I'm most likely going to need some more medication, as they only gave me enough for a couple of days. Also, would you call the dentist and make an appointment with him? Apparently, my jaw is all screwed up, and I need him to take a look at it. Thanks, Mom. I really appreciate it."

"That's no problem. I'll let them both know that it's because of the accident, and hopefully they will both get you right in."

"That's great, Mom. Thank you. Okay, it's about 11:30. Richard should be here any time. Do you want me to call you when we leave here?"

"No, that will be fine. I'll just plan on seeing you both around dinnertime. I did ask Richard to go by and take a look at the car, so you will be able to get your things out of it."

"Oh, good. Yeah, I need my suitcase from the trunk. Oh… there's a knock on my door. I bet it's Richard; hold on a minute."

I put down the phone and dashed to the door. Peeking through the peephole, I saw my brother. Opening the door, I said, "Mom's on the phone. Let me tell her you're here."

I picked up the receiver. "Mom, Richard's here. We are going to take off now. I need to go down and pay the final bill at the front desk. Then off to see the car, I guess. I love you, and we'll see you in about three hours or so. Bye, Mom."

"You two be careful coming home. Goodbye."

As soon as I hang up, my brother piped up with, "Boy, you look like shit."

"Gee, thanks, Richard. It's good to see you, too. You try getting run over by a semi-truck, and let's see how good you fare. Let me grab my purse and we can go take care of the bill and get the hell out of here. I want to go home!"

"All right. You go take care of the bill, and I'll pull the van up to the entry."

Richard had an old Volkswagen van. As we left the room, he went one way out to the parking lot, and I headed for the front desk. I handed my key to the attendant.

"Hello," I said. "I'm checking out of my room now."

The attendant said, "That total comes to $155. Would you like that all on the credit card you provided at time of check-in?"

"Yes, that all goes on it. Do you need to see it again?"

"No, there's no need, thank you. I hope you were comfortable with your stay here."

"As comfortable as I could get. Thank you for everything you did to help me. I certainly appreciate it."

He handed me the receipt to sign.

"Thanks again. You have a good day."

"Yes, thank you for staying with us. I hope you get to feeling better soon."

As I walked away from the front desk, I noticed Richard's van right outside the door. I got in and asked,

 "So, where are we headed to first?"

"I need to go by the sheriff's office for a record of the accident. Then we need to find the car. I have an address for it. Maybe someone at the police station will know where it is and how to get there."

We drove off and it wasn't too long before we were at the CHP's office. I waited in the van while Richard went in to talk with them. He was not gone very long.

Richard got back in the van and said, "The car is at an auto shop in Lakehead. They will mail us the accident report in a few days. So, off to Lakehead it is."

The entire drive up there, which only took about thirty minutes, not a word was said. The silence was deafening. He didn't even have any music on. I could tell this was not going to be a joyride home. For starters, his van seats were very uncomfortable, and given the age and style of the vehicle, I was not going to enjoy this trip at all. I could feel every bump. It was most uncomfortable.

Once we got close to Lakehead, I saw where the accident happened. The snow was not as thick where the car had been. You could still see the imprints of the tow truck and the emergency vehicles that had been parked there. We soon crossed over that bridge where I had made the sign of the cross, asking to get to Redding safely. I guess my prayer was heard because there was no logical reason I should be alive right now. Let alone hurt, rather minimally.

That was the affirmation I needed to know that Angel Bob, once again, had a very busy day.

Thank you again, Angel Bob. You are going to be hearing a lot of that from me now.

Wow, more than three months ago—three months and three days to be exact—I was almost killed in the MGM.

Geez, I can't believe how fortunate I feel right now.

I felt bad for the car in front of me. There were four ladies in that car, and one of them didn't go home. She was killed. The others, I heard, were in rather bad shape.

You know, I don't even remember seeing that car in front of me. I knew they were there because I was driving in their tire tracks. I watched that semi from the top of the hill all the way to me, and I do not remember seeing him hit their car. What tricks the mind can play on you when you are abruptly taken from a normal situation and thrown into a highly stressful circumstance. As I said before, it was in such slow motion, it was almost unbelievable. It did give me enough time, or things just flew through my mind so fast, that I came up with a solution as opposed to just sitting there waiting for impact.

Thank God and Angel Bob for giving me the foresight to let go of the wheel and lay down on that seat. I remember as a child, I had a premonition about laying down in the front seat of a car, and I never understood what it meant. I believe I understand now.

Richard pulled into Lakehead, and we found the auto shop where the Maverick was taken. An attendant came out."Hello, folks, what can I help you with today?"

"Hello," Richard said. "Here's the title to the blue Ford Maverick that was brought in a couple days ago. We are the owners and would like to see the car. My sister also needs to get into the trunk for her suitcase."

"That sounds fine," the attendant said. "You can park right here, and the Maverick is right inside the fence there. I'll get the key so we can get into the trunk."

"Thank you. We'll meet you over there."

Richard and I walk around the fence to find the poor Maverick.

"Damnation!" I exclaimed. "That looks horrible! I can't believe I was in that car."

"That truck sure did a number on it. We won't be driving this car again."

"Richard, once I get my suitcase, can we get out of here as quick as possible? My stomach isn't feeling too good right now. I feel like I want to throw up."

"Well, if you're going to do that, please do it before getting back in my van."

"Gee, thanks. I'll make sure not to puke in your car."

The man came over to us and unlocked the truck, opening it to reveal my suitcase. This poor suitcase had seen as much shit as I had in the last three months. I think it was time to retire this suitcase. I wasn't sure if it had brought me bad luck that things keep happening to me—or good luck because I was landing on my feet each time.

I only have you to thank, Bob. You and God.

I approached the suitcase and opened it, just enough to see that my pipe and bag of weed were in there. I did not dream up that hippie chick. Even if no one else saw her, she was there. Not for long, but long enough to hide the evidence. That was the last thing the officials needed to know, that I was smoking pot at the time of the accident. It wouldn't have made a difference. I still had no traction and couldn't get out of his way. I was trapped, pot or not.

"Thank you very much for letting me get my belongings," I told the attendant. "You have a good day."

I walked off to the van, opening the back door and crawling in. If I had to ride back to Medford in silence, I was going to do it laying down.

Richard got in the van, started it up, and we were on our way again.

I told him, "I'm going to lay down and see if I can sleep for the rest of the ride home."

"That's fine. Hope you're comfortable."

I did manage to sleep for most of the ride home. At least it went by quickly. *Now I can see Dad again.* As Richard was pulling into the driveway, I am ready to hop out and run to my father.

"I can't wait to see Dad!" I exclaimed.

"Well, you're going to have to wait a little longer because he's not in there," Richard said. "They took him to the hospital yesterday."

"What the hell? Why didn't Mom tell me? I have a right to know where my father is."

I stormed into the house wearing my cream-colored neck brace. As soon as I saw Mom, I said, "Why didn't you tell me Dad went back to the hospital?"

"There wasn't anything you could have done from there but worry," she said, "and I didn't want you sitting there stewing over your father."

I was furious. "And what do you think I thought of most of the time I was there? It was Dad and how he was doing. You kept telling me he was doing fine. You could very easily have told me he was back there."

"I'm sorry, I should have told you, but I didn't want you to worry."

"Do we get to go up and see him?"

"Harriet and I have already been there for the day. He's resting now."

"Well, I want to go up there first thing in the morning tomorrow."

Mom changed the subject. It was around six o'clock now, almost dinnertime.

Richard asked, "So, what is there for dinner? It's been a long day for me."

"Oh, and it hasn't been a long couple of days for me?"

Our mother snapped: "Now, just stop it, you two. The last thing I want to hear is you two arguing."

"Sorry, Mom," I said. "I've been a little stressed out the last couple of days. My whole body is sore. Can I go for a short drive in your car? I need some fresh air."

"Sure, just don't be gone long. I want you here at the house."

"Okay, I'll be gone half an hour."

I took my suitcase back to the den and put my pipe and bag of pot in my purse. Back to the dining room, I got Mom's car keys from the wooden bowl on the desk, grabbed my purse, and headed out the garage door. In her car and out the driveway, I headed to Cherry Lane.

I drove to the south side of the hill and pulled over in a spot where you can see the twinkling lights of the city below. I opened my purse, taking out my pipe and pot. I filled up the pipe and just sat there, watching the lights dance in the night air.

Well, this is an interesting "how do you do?" Dad's back in the hospital, I'm in a neck brace, and my mother is in stitches. You know, now that I think about it. I haven't seen her cry. Is she really that strong, or was she just taught that you don't show your emotions? Hell, I'm sitting here crying about it 'cause I know it's coming. Dad is soon to be no longer with us. How do I get through this? It's too hard to fathom life without Dad.

I smoked one more bowl and then finished my drive around the hill. I aimed the car toward home, and it seemed to get there on automatic pilot, as I was thinking about life after Dad. I pulled into the driveway and into the garage. It was easy to tell where to stop so you knew the car was all the way in. Dad had hung a tennis ball from the rafters so Mom would know that when she hit the ball, she could stop. Dad had rigged up a pretty good system for her.

I got out of the car, leaving all the windows rolled down. As I approached the door, I hit the button to close the garage. In the family/dining room, Mom and Hat were watching an episode of *Magnum* PI with Tom Selleck. What a handsome hunk of a man!

I knew not to talk while they were watching, so I walked over to the desk to deposit the keys in their bowl. I then made my way to the freezer to get some ice cream. I packed a bowl full of vanilla and poured a heavy amount of Hershey's Chocolate Syrup over the top, while adding banana slices. No, I didn't have the munchies.

I sat at the dining table to eat while watching *Magnum*. It had been a long day. Once again, I was not only physically worn out, but my emotions were completely drained. After I finished my ice cream, I took the bowl to the sink, rinsed it out, and placed it in the dishwasher.

"Mom, I'm going to go lay down on the couch and hopefully go to sleep. You two have a good night. Enjoy your show."

"Good night, Judy," they replied.

First I went to the bathroom, brushed my teeth and washed my face. It felt so good to use a real toothbrush again. After using the facilities, I washed up and headed out to the couch. I had one of my old pillows from when I lived here, and half of the hospital blanket that Mom had cut in two for Dad. It was too big in one piece. Now it was the right size for a single person to use. It was surprisingly warm. That was all I needed to feel close to Dad. This was his blanket that he had used here at the house, but they had left it behind this last time when they took him away.

It took some doing as I lay there listening to the television show coming from the other room. I could kind of follow along with the dialog. As always, Magnum got the bad guy with great panache. Fade into theme music and cut to commercial. The evening news followed, but by the time Johnny Carson was on, I was out cold.

I woke up at about 7:30 to Mom and Hat talking. I couldn't quite make out what they were saying. It was as if they were purposefully speaking in a low tone so I could not hear what they were saying. I laid there for another hour dozing off and on. Finally, by 8:30, I had to go to the bathroom, and once I was up, that was it.

I got new clothes out to put on. I still didn't know if Mom was able to get the blood stains out of my favorite shirt. I would have to ask. For now, a t-shirt and my zip-up hoodie worked just fine. Thank goodness I had brought about three different pairs of jeans with me. Now, I was down to two until I do laundry.

I went to the kitchen, saying my "good mornings" as I entered. Still a little groggy, I needed some caffeine to wake up completely. Unfortunately, I do not drink coffee, so I went to the fridge to find myself a Pepsi. I cracked it open and took a nice, big, cold drink. It tasted so good first thing in the morning with the bubbles dancing over my tongue and down my throat. I then got my bowl of Cheerios and sat at the table with Mom and Hat while the morning news was on the television. They had stopped talking since I walked in the room. It seemed rather odd to me. I got the feeling they were keeping something from me, but I couldn't figure out what it could possibly be. After eating, I put my bowl and spoon in the dishwasher, retreating to the living room where I folded up my sheet and blanket, setting them neatly on the pillow. Then I sat on the green leather sofa that they had moved to Dad's room. When I returned from Redding, all the furniture was back in its place, except for Dad's bed. The hospital bed was gone, and Mom had put her bed back in there, but there was no sign of Dad's bed.

The three of us were still sitting there an hour later when the phone rang. Mom walked to the desk to answer. She didn't say much, actually nothing at all, she just nodded her head, finally saying, "Thank you."

She turned to us, calling for Richard to come out to the kitchen. We were all there.

"That was the hospital calling," Mom said. "We all need to get to the hospital now. Except you, Judy. You stay here."

"No! If Dad is dying, I want to be with him, too! Why do I need to stay?"

My mother said, "I don't want your father to know that you were in a car accident. I don't want him seeing you with that neck brace on. I want him to go in peace."

"Mom, I can take the neck brace off!"

"No, you stay here, and that's that." She got her purse as Richard and Harriet followed her out to her car. I watched out the dining room window as Mom's gold Chevrolet Impala moved down the street without me.

How could she do that to me? It's not fair that I don't get to go say goodbye to my own father.

Needless to say, I was immensely upset with her. I paced back and forth between the kitchen and the living room while the TV was still on.

Before I knew it, they were all back. They weren't gone but maybe thirty minutes. Mom walked through the door first and looked at me saying, "It's done. He's out of pain now."

"Dad's dead?"

"Yes, Judy, your father is gone and at peace, out of pain now."

I couldn't say anything. No words would come out of my mouth. I didn't know if it was the shock of hearing Dad was gone, or if I were still so very upset with Mom, that I just couldn't bring myself to speak to her or anyone.

I left the room and went into the bathroom in my parent's bedroom. I put the seat down and just sat there.

It's not fair. I'm only 28. I still need my dad.

I started crying and couldn't stop. I was in there a good twenty minutes, bawling my eyes out. I pulled myself together, splashed some cold water on my face, and dried it with one of Dad's towels.

I left the bathroom and headed for the den. I couldn't smoke anything right now, so I reached into my suitcase to find my black fuzzy booties. I had tucked away the vial of coke with my straw, mirror, and razor. I carried the booties back into the bathroom, locking the door behind me. I sat again, putting the mirror on my lap to chop up a couple medium lines of coke. I snorted them down and cleaned up my mess, putting everything back in my booties. Then I deposited them in my suitcase.

I went into the front bathroom to check my nose to make sure I had no trace of white showing. That would be a sure giveaway. Maybe Mom wouldn't catch it, but my nosey brother would.

I don't need that. I just need to numb myself so I can get through this day.

It was Friday, February 27th. The worst three months of my life.

I pretty much hung out in Mom and Dad's room. The small television was still in there, and I really wanted to be alone. Everyone else was in the family room except my brother; he, of course, was out golfing. How could he possibly go golfing the day his father died?

He is a strange one. I never will understand him. Mom's voice carries faintly into the bedroom. I figured she was making arrangements for Dad. I didn't want to be around to hear that, so I turned up the TV volume just a little more.

Since it was Friday, the service for Dad wouldn't be until Tuesday. Mom had arranged a little something at the church.

On Monday, I had the two doctor's appointments that Mom had made for me. First, I would see her physician to give me a once-over. I did get a few more pain pills from him and a month's worth of Valium, but he told me to make sure to see my own doctor when I returned to Los Angeles. I went straight from that appointment to my dentist.

"Well, hello again, Judy," he said. "I hope you had a smooth time of it after I pulled your wisdom teeth."

"Hello Dr. Bendicks. They healed up nicely. But I'm having an issue with my jaw."

"Yes, I understand you had a little run-in with a semi-truck. You are one lucky lady to have walked away from that. Now, let's take a look at your jaw."

He had me opening and closing my mouth. Each time, my jaw hurt like a son-of-a-gun, popping in and out of its socket. The hinge-like bones that connect your skull and jawbone are called the temporomandibular joint. Injuries can trigger a painful disorder known as TMJ.

It gave me the worst headaches. Apparently, it was out of place and there really wasn't anything he could do about it now. He said that eventually it would pop back in and stay there. But he couldn't say how long that would be. I felt he wasn't that much help, so I made an appointment with my dentist in LA. Hopefully he could help.

By the time the service rolled around on Tuesday, the funeral home had some issues, and Dad was still not cremated, so he did not make it to his church service. There were only a handful of people there. Jean, his secretary, attended with her daughter. A few of the neighbors had come, along with about a dozen of the attorneys that Dad had worked with in town. A few colleagues and friends had driven down from Portland for the service as well.

I don't really remember much of the service. It's strange, but the only thing I do remember was thinking that I would get to ride in a limousine for the first time, but the car the funeral home sent for us was just a Continental. Nothing special.

After the service, we came back to the house, just the family. We all wanted to be alone. Richard took off again for the golf course, while Mom and Hat were in the family/dining room. I went on back to what was once my bedroom and closed the door. I didn't want to see or talk to anyone. I was in there for the better part of the day, crying and sleeping. Around five o'clock, Mom knocked on my door and came in.

"You should come on out to the kitchen and eat something," she said. "You haven't eaten all day."

"I'm not hungry. But I will come on out. Give me a few minutes."

She left, closing the door behind her. I got up and opened my closet door, setting my mirror on top of the dresser that was inside. That way, if anyone were to open the door, they would not see what I was doing. I quickly chopped up a couple of lines, snorting them and returning everything to my suitcase. If I had to make an appearance, I want to be numb.

I went out to join Harriet and Mom. Mother had a tuna sandwich sitting on the dining table with a glass of milk for me. I sat down and started to eat half of it. Odd, but it had no flavor.

"Mom, do you have some chips?"

"Yes, dear. They're in the cupboard above the fridge."

As I reached up and got them down, Mom continued, "I was talking with Richard before he went to play golf. He is going to drive you back to LA and be there for the internment. He would like to leave tomorrow morning, if you're ready to go."

I swallowed a bite of sandwich and said, "Oh, no offense, Mom, but I am more than ready to go home. I need to take care of my bills, and I miss my cat. Will the funeral home have Dad's ashes ready for us to take back with us?"

She shook her head. "I doubt it. Your brother wants to get an early start in the morning. So, if they don't have him ready today, they will have to ship him down to you."

She got up to get more coffee and continued, "I have been in touch with the cemetery, it's Woodlawn Cemetery in Santa Monica. You've been there before when we've taken flowers there. I will make sure you have the address."

"Okay, Mom." I should have been paying more attention to what she was saying, but I didn't care at the moment.

I'm empty inside. There is a huge hole in my heart. It's selfish of me to still want him here with me, but I'm glad he is out of pain now.

That was hard watching him go through what he did. My father was one very strong man. It hurt too much to see him fade away into the distance.

The front door opened. My brother was home from golfing. He saw me and said, "I hope you get a good night's sleep tonight, because I want to be on the road by six, seven at the latest."

"Don't worry. If I'm not completely awake, I'll just lay in the back of the van and go back to sleep."

We all ate dinner, watched a little television, and went to bed. I slept in my old room while Richard slept on the couch in the living room.

Mom was the first one up the next morning. I could smell the robust aroma of the pot of coffee she put on. Even though I don't drink coffee, I do like the smell of it. The taste is too bitter for my liking. I heard Richard get up and go into the kitchen. They were in there talking. I figured I would lay in bed until one of them came to wake me up. Why get up any earlier than I need to? Sure enough, about a half hour later, here came Mom to the door.

"Judy. It's time to get up. Your brother wants to leave in about thirty minutes."

"Okay, Mom. I'm getting up." She closed the door so I could get dressed. I got up, made my bed, then looked for my most comfortable jeans to wear on the way home. I put on a Portland Trailblazer t-shirt with my Dodger zip-up hoodie.

The night before, I had chopped up the last of my coke and put it all back into its vial. That way, I could just dip into it with my little spoon and wouldn't need the mirror or straw. I knew this would be a winner of a trip back to LA with my brother. It was well understood by each of us that we didn't really care for one another. I took a couple little hits and was ready to face the world—me and my lovely neck brace.

I went to the kitchen and poured some Cheerios, and sat at the table to eat. When I was finished, I went to the bathroom to brush my teeth and pee one last time. It wasn't long before I was ready for the trip back.

"Okay, Richard. I'm set. Let's get this show on the road."

"It's about time. I'll go warm up the van," Richard said, getting up to leave the house.

I turned to my mother.

"Now, Mom, I don't want you to worry about us at all. Richard's a good driver, and really, how fast can you go in a VW van? I'll make sure to call you when we get home to my apartment. Are you going to be okay?"

"Yes, dear. Don't you worry about me. I'm going to be just fine. Hat is coming over for coffee this morning, so I won't be alone."

Just as Mom spoke, in walked Hat from the garage.

"Good morning, you two," Hat said. Then she turned to me. "I talked to Richard out in the driveway. So, you are all ready to go home?"

"Oh, more than you know. I really miss Turkey, and can't wait to cuddle up with him again." (My cat, if you didn't catch that earlier.)

I gave Hat a hug as I said, "Please take care of Mom. I love you very much. You take care."

I turned to give Mom a hug and kiss, and said, "I love you, Mom. Now, please don't worry about Richard and me. I will call you as soon as we get to LA, about seven tonight. Bye."

I picked up my suitcase and purse, heading to the garage door. Once I got out to the van, I threw my suitcase into the back. Mom and Hat had followed me out to wave goodbye to us. Richard was chomping at the bit to get going. If he had his way, he would have left an hour ago. We waved goodbye to Mom and Hat as we backed out of the driveway and headed down the street.

The ride was just as I had thought: long, quiet, and boring. Before I knew it, though, we were driving past Lakehead and crossing the little bridge just before the accident spot. I was getting very anxious, not wanting to go any farther.

"This is it," I said. "We're about to go around the hill where the accident happened."

As we rounded that corner, it was like it was going to happen all over again. I started to give Richard a play-by-play rendition of the crash. My brother was driving the speed limit, allowing me to realize how little time I had to think of what I could possibly do to escape the semi barreling straight at me. By the time we reached the top of the hill where the semi started to lose control, I was still talking about how it was about to hit me sideways.

I finished my story, which I don't think he really cared about hearing, and turned to him, saying, "I'm going to crawl into the back and lay down. I don't feel so good."

With that said, I made my way to the back. Richard had a small mattress back there, so I did have something to lay on that made it somewhat comfortable. That was as comfortable as I could get. My muscles felt much better than a week ago. I didn't hurt quite as much. My jaw, however, was giving me a hard time, along with, this neck brace that I was told to wear for at least a month. I thought that was a little excessive, but when I went without it for a few hours, my neck would get very sore.

I tried to sleep most of the way, mainly to avoid needing potty stops. Richard was all about getting there as quickly as possible, with very few stops. We finally rolled into Studio City at about 6:30 that evening, right at rush hour. Oh, what a joy. Before I knew it, we were at my exit and turning the corner to my apartment. Richard found a parking place out front. Once parked, I grabbed my suitcase and purse, fumbling through it to find my apartment key.

I headed into the building, stopping at the mailboxes to empty mine. By this time, Richard was next to me with his golf clubs and tote bag. We rounded the stairs, going up to the second floor, and down the long, bland beige hallway to my front door, which was nicely painted red. As I was putting the key in the keyhole, I heard Turkey on the other side of the door. He knew Mom was home.

We both entered. I went in first, pointing to the couch. "This is your bed, Richard. I'll get you a pillow and blanket in a bit. We need to call Mom."

I went to my room to put down the suitcase. Then I picked up Turkey to give him some love. We headed back into the living room, where I grabbed the phone and dialed Mom's number.

"Hi, Mom. We're here safe and sound. You can relax now."

"That's good. How was the drive?"

"Long. I slept most of the way. Well, I just called to let you know. I'm really tired from the trip. I'll talk to you on Sunday. I love you, Mom. Bye."

"I love you, too. Goodbye."

The next morning came quickly, with sunbeams shining in my bedroom window. I heard Richard stirring in the kitchen. I got up, went to the bathroom, then headed to the kitchen in my pajamas.

"Let me guess. You're going golfing?"

"Good morning to you, too, smart ass."

"Which golf course?"

"Griffith Park. You know that's my favorite."

"Yeah, it is beautiful there," I said as I opened a cupboard door, pulling out a key ring. I handed it to Richard.

"Here's the spare house key, so you can come and go if I'm not here."

"Okay. Thank you. I'll see you later." He walked across the living room, picked up his golf clubs, and headed out the door. I heard him close and lock the door behind him.

It wasn't long before I found myself pacing from the kitchen to the couch, and into the bedroom, where from my nightstand I picked up one of the Polaroid pictures Mom had taken of Dad at Christmas. I gazed at him, sitting on their sofa beside the Christmas tree. Then I took my right pointer finger, kissed it, and touched Dad's face. Holding the picture tight to my chest, I headed back to the kitchen again.

I couldn't stop thinking of Dad. I found it very hard to accept the fact that he was really gone. I leaned my back up against the wall, next to the refrigerator, gripping his picture to my heart while looking down the narrow kitchen and out the dining room window. I stood there, staring at the top of a lush green palm tree that was ever-so-gently swaying with the breeze. My eyes were fixed on it for a good five minutes, while tears started to well up.

Before I knew it, crying became full-on sobbing. My body slid down the wall until I was sitting on the cold, hard linoleum floor. It seemed like I was there forever, as my sobbing turned to a low, painful whimper, and my body slumped all the way down. Soon, I found myself curled up in the fetal position.

I must have been there for a good thirty minutes or so. I had stopped the whimpering and just laid there motionless.

"Get the hell up!"

This order came from a voice that I did not recognize.

Was it Angel Bob? Who else would be jarring me out of my deep, depressed state of mind?

I shot up like a bullet. Then I took a Dr. Pepper from the fridge, opened it, and took it to the bedroom with me.

As I set the soda on the nightstand, I also opened the cupboard, reached in behind the metal plate, and pulled out a full gram of coke. I figured that, and some smoke, would numb me up for a good week. I went through the routine of only pouring out enough for a couple small lines, chopping it, etc. This was my way of justifying it taking longer to use it, if I had to prepare it each time I wanted a hit. I can justify about anything, I'm very good at it, and it comes from years of practice.

I went into the workroom to get a jar of smoke, sat down at my worktable, and rolled a good dozen joints. Five went into my cute silver cigarette case, and the others remained in the jar with the pot for later. Despite doing some coke, I had no ambition whatsoever. My depression gripped so tight on my soul, it was hard to move. I didn't care to draw. I had no pretty thoughts at the moment.

Thank goodness my boss had no work for me right now, as I was still wearing the neck brace and suffering with headaches.

I did find the energy to call my physician for a check-up. I also called my dentist in Burbank for another look at my jaw. I was not happy with the diagnosis I received in Medford.

Next, I burrowed through my purse to find the name and phone number of the shrink Pamela had given me. I had written it on a white index card that I had found at my mother's house. I picked up the receiver and dialed the number.

"Good morning, this is Dr. Jacks' office. How may I help you?"

"Hello. I was given Dr. Jacks' information from a friend, and I really need to see a shrink, excuse me, a psychiatrist. Is he taking any new patients?"

"What is your current problem?" the receptionist asked.

"Well, about three and a half months ago, I was stuck in the MGM Grand fire in Las Vegas. Since then, I have been run over by a semi-truck, and my father just passed away. I believe I need to talk to someone."

The receptionist said, "Oh, my. I would say you're probably right. The soonest I can get you in is in two weeks. Will that work for you?"

"Yes, please."

"How about Friday, March 20th, at 1 p.m.? Will that work for you?"

"Yes, that will be fine, unless you get a cancelation. Probably the sooner I can get in, the better. I have never been this depressed in my whole life."

The receptionist asked, "Do you feel that you're suicidal?"

"No. I would never do harm to myself or anyone, for that matter."

"Well, all right then. We will see you Friday, March 20th at 1 p.m.

You have a good couple of weeks. Goodbye now."

"Thank you. Goodbye."

Wow, that was interesting. I had never seen a shrink before. *Will I really have to lie down on a couch? Maybe I got a good one, since he's in Beverly Hills. This should be covered on my Motion Picture Health Insurance—I hope. Well, I need it, whether it's covered or not.*

I am about to lose it. I'm going to have to hold myself together, at least while Richard is here. I certainly don't want him to see me in such a mess.

Now what? I took my cigarette case into the bedroom, turned on the television, and lit a joint. I had absolutely no desire to do anything. I had to give it to Richard, at least he had something to do that he enjoyed and didn't seem all that upset about Dad's passing. My Aunt Hat always said Richard was an "odd one," ever since he was small.

I didn't see much of Richard for the next week while we were waiting for Dad's internment the following Thursday. Which was totally fine with me. I really wanted to be alone, anyway.

The days went by slow, but also rather quickly, if that makes any sense to you. Now, it was Tuesday and I noticed that we were missing something. Dad hadn't arrived yet.

When Richard returned from golf for the day I asked him, "When was Dad supposed to have been here? Shouldn't he be here by now? It's been a week. The funeral home has had plenty of time to cremate him and get him down to us. So, where the hell is he?"

My brother answered, "Don't get so worked up about it. I'm sure he'll show up tomorrow. Give it time."

"If you haven't noticed," I snapped, "his internment is the day after tomorrow. We can't exactly go through with it if he's not here."

"Judy, go smoke a joint and chill out. There's nothing to worry about. He'll be here."

"Well, I'm really glad you're so sure of that. I'll be in my room smoking, so it doesn't bother you, your allergies and all. So, watch what you want, I've got the small TV in my room."

"Good, chill out. It will be fine."

I got a dish of Rocky Road ice cream, which became my mainstay for the week, because I was not interested in eating anything else. I headed to my room, closing the door behind me. Sitting up on the bed, I ate my ice cream, which was creamy and chunky all at the same time. And I loved the marshmallow part. Then I light a joint. Thank goodness this was relaxing me enough to finally unwind. I felt like my head had been spinning like a top the last couple of days, wondering where Dad was. Off to sleep I drifted until morning.

By the time I got up, dressed and went into the other room, Richard had already left to golf. Geez, what time did he take off? I certainly didn't hear him. I returned to my bedroom and pulled out the coke vial, which had lasted me exactly a week—not bad.

However, if Dad didn't show up soon, I would be getting into the other vial I had stashed away.

Next thing I knew, it was ten o'clock.

Let's do another line.

At noon, I opened the front door, even though I hadn't heard a knock. I found nothing. No package, no Dad, no anything. I was getting exceedingly anxious and very disturbed that Dad had not been delivered yet. I did another small line, and by this time, I was chain-smoking my joints. It was one in the afternoon and I couldn't take it any longer.

I looked up the phone number to the funeral home. Hopefully I could track down Dad's ashes without having to call Mom. I dialed.

"You've reached the funeral home. How may I help you?"

"Hello, this is Judy Bohning calling, and I need to speak to someone who would know the whereabouts of my father. His name is Wallace W. Bohning."

"Just a moment, I'll transfer you to our Funeral Director."

I was put on hold for several minutes, listening to godawful elevator music.

"Hello, Miss Bohning. This is the funeral director. What can I help you with today?"

"Um, yes. Could you possibly tell me where my father is, please?"

"Are you saying that you haven't received him yet?"

"That is exactly what I am saying," I said, allowing my tone to convey my anger. "His internment is tomorrow, and without the Guest of Honor, it's going to be a little difficult to bury the man!"

The director can obviously tell that I am a touch on the upset side. I was holding my temper and watching my tongue, but it was not easy to be polite at this given moment.

"Just one moment, Miss Bohning. Let me go check on when he was shipped out. I'll be right back," he said before putting me on hold.

That damn elevator music again. Wasn't it bad enough that your loved one had passed away, and now they made you suffer even more with elevator music? This seemed to be taking longer than it should.

I was pacing the living room, wearing a path in the lovely green shag carpeting. Finally, he came back to the phone. "Yes, Miss Bohning, you should have received him by now. We mailed him out to you a week ago."

"You… mailed… him?" I asked in the calmest voice I could muster.

Then my anger burst out: "ARE YOU FUCKING CRAZY???"

My voice got even louder:

"YOU FUCKING MAILED HIM!!!!! What? UPS or FedEx weren't available that day, or did my mother buy the discount package?"

I took a breath and continued: "You do realize that his internment is tomorrow at two in the afternoon. He better be there, or you will be hearing from me again. Don't bother talking with my mother. I'm the one in LA that has to deal with everything and undo this, so people don't show up for no reason."

I took another breath.

"If I were you," I warned, "I would do the best you can to try and track him down. You have my number. Please call me if you find out anything. Goodbye!" I slammed the receiver into the phone cradle. It was now three in the afternoon and I was still chain-smoking. The patio sliding glass door was open so the smoke would blow out, plus I had a couple of vanilla candles burning to attempt to cover the pot smell.

Richard came in, and before he had time to put down his golf clubs, I was on him.

"Do you have any idea what that idiot funeral home did?"

Richard just looked at me, waiting for me to tell him.

"They mailed Dad to us. They have absolutely no idea where he is. What are we going to do tomorrow?"

"It's no big deal," my brother said. "Just call the people that are coming and tell them you'll be in touch when we find him."

"Well, that's easy for you to say," I snapped. "I tell the Griffins and Jimmie tells Mom. I don't want Mom getting upset. You don't even sound the least bit upset that they have lost our father!!!"

Richard was calm. "There's nothing we can do about it now. We'll just have to wait and see if he shows up tomorrow morning."

"Well, they've got until about eleven o'clock at the latest to get him here before I will have to call people. I'm going to get some ice cream and go to bed. This has been a very upsetting day for me."

I got my Rocky Road and headed to the bedroom, closing the door. I was just beside myself. I didn't dare call Mom and tell her this. I didn't want to upset her any more than necessary. I found something on television to watch, smoked a couple of joints, then I was out for the night.

By the time the next morning rolled around, I woke up earlier than usual. I was very anxious to find my father. I was in and out of the shower very quickly, putting on my house jeans and a t-shirt with a red plaid, flannel long-sleeve shirt. It was about 7:30 when I went out to the kitchen.

Where's my brother? Has he seriously gone golfing this morning? I can't believe him.

If he's going to zone out playing golf, I'm going to numb myself with a hit of coke.

After that, I lit a joint and started pacing. I needed to do something to keep my mind off my father not being here yet. I went into my workroom and sat at my drawing table, smoking my joint. I tried drawing, but nothing wanted to come out. I sat there for a good twenty minutes hoping something will come to me, but not even my doodling was any good.

Obviously, that wasn't working, so I attempted to clean the house. In the kitchen, I rinsed a handful of dishes in the sink and put them in the dishwasher. I scrubbed down everything, even wiping down the front of the appliances, the fridge, dishwasher, and stove. I went as far as mopping the floor.

It might as well be clean if I should find myself down there again.

By this time, it was about 8:30, and the only thing I could think of was to try and get in touch with someone at the Post Office. I looked up the number and fortunately, Sally, the window clerk who usually helps me, answered the phone.

"Hello, USPS, this is Sally. How may I help you?"

"Oh, Sally, am I glad it's you. This is Judy Bohning. I have a bit of a situation here. The funeral home in Medford, Oregon mailed my father's ashes to me last week. I have yet to receive them and his internment is this afternoon. Is there any way you can check to see if a box from Medford has arrived for me, or if one has been put aside? Is there anything you can find out? I would really appreciate it!"

Sally answered, "Let me put you on hold for a minute and I'll see what I can find out."

"That's great. Thank you so much."

Dang, there's that damn elevator music again. Does everyone subscribe to this stuff?

Sally was gone a good five minutes, during which time I wore a new path in my shag carpeting.

"Hello, Judy? I don't see anything laying around for you, and your carrier left hours ago. There's no way I can tell if he has it with him or not. What time does he usually deliver your mail?"

"It depends," I said. "Somewhere between ten and noon. I need to leave for the cemetery in Santa Monica by 12:30 at the latest."

Sally said, "It sounds like you will make it as long as the package came in this morning. Good luck to you, Judy. Let me know how it turns out."

"Thank you very much, Sally. I certainly will. You have a good day. Bye."

I hung up the phone for a brief instant, then picked it up again to call the funeral home.

"You've reached the funeral home. How may I help you?"

"Yes," I said. "Is the funeral director available?"

"Yes. May I tell him who is calling?"

"Yes. This is Judy Bohning."

She put me on hold with that same music. Fortunately, it was not long.

"Good morning, Ms. Bohning," said the funeral director. "Have you received him yet?"

"As a matter of fact, NO! I have not. Do you have any idea as to his whereabouts?"

"I'm very sorry for all this inconvenience," he said, "but I was not able to find out anything as to where he could be right now. You do have my sympathies, and I do hope he shows up on time."

"Well, if he doesn't," I snapped, "I will be telling my mother about this, and I will expect you to not only give her your sincere apology, but I will hope that you have your business in mind and refund her several hundred dollars for our inconvenience. Thank you. Goodbye."

I needed to hang up that phone before I got extremely rude.

I am just livid right now. Well, shit! Let's do another line or two and start to get ready, just in case he shows up.

I put on my makeup and curl my hair, thinking that if he didn't show up and I have gotten ready for nothing, I would not be happy. By the time I finished, it was pushing ten o'clock.

I walked out to the living room and down the entry hall to the front door. I opened it, hoping that the postal carrier had knocked and I had not heard it. But sadly, that was not the case. There was nothing out there. The postal carrier would have to bring it up to the apartment, because Dad wouldn't fit in my mail slot.

As I went back into the kitchen to look for something to drink, I heard a knock at the door.

Thank God, Dad's here. I practically ran to the door, opening it.

"Thanks, I forgot my key," my brother said.

"Are you serious, going golfing the morning of Dad's burial? That is, if he ever gets here."

"What, he hasn't shown up yet?"

"NO! He hasn't. I've been calling all over, looking for him."

Richard said, "Well, there's nothing I could have done about anything, so why not go golfing? At least I'm not sitting around here going crazy over the situation. Geez, Judy, chill the hell out."

"I'll chill the hell out when Dad shows up."

"Well, at least smoke a joint," Richard said. "Do something besides getting all upset over something you can't control."

"Gee, I'm so glad you're so calm about all of this," I said. "I'm going to my room."

In my room with the door closed, I thought, I *might as well get dressed so I'm ready... that is, if he shows up.* I got my good, dry-cleaned jeans out of the closet and put them on. Maybe I could pair them with a nice black silk blouse and my black ankle boots. I had my good black coat to wear in case it was chilly out there. Santa Monica, for those who don't know, is on the ocean in Los Angeles, so it tends to be chilly this time of year.

About a half hour later, Richard knocked on my door.

"Yeah, come on in," I said.

"Your package has arrived," my brother said, standing in the doorway, holding the box of Dad's ashes.

"THANK GOD!!!" I shouted. "Are you sure it's him? Is it from the funeral home?"

"Yes. It's him. Now can you please chill the fuck out?"

It was a Thursday and I was thinking about the traffic to Santa Monica this time of the day.

"Well, Richard. It's a little after eleven. Even though it's not a Friday, it's still heading towards the beach. If we need to be there by two, we should probably leave here at 12:30. No, let's leave at 12:15. Make sure we don't have any issues. I'll drive, since I know where we're going."

"That's fine by me," my brother said. "I hate LA traffic."

"Okay, we have a little while before we need to leave, so I'm going to go relax now that I know Dad's safe."

I sat on the bed with my feet stretched out. Turkey hopped up to cuddle a bit. I lit a joint and sat back to chill. I didn't even bother turning on the television. I just wanted to hear the quiet of my room. I wanted to think about the good times that Dad and I shared.

I'll never forget about the time we were staying over at the coast when I was maybe ten or eleven. I guess Dad had told Mom that he would stop smoking. Actually, I really believe it was the other way around; Mom told Dad he was going to quit. Anyway, we were taking a walk on the beach, just Dad and me. He pulls out a sucker and says to me, "This is yours if you don't tell your mother I smoked a cigarette."

"Don't worry, Dad. I won't say anything."

Dad was my hero. He was my super star. Now I felt so lost without him here. Knowing that I would never hear his voice again. I would never get good advice from him anymore. He was very wise. I just missed him. Plain and simple.

It's time. Richard came to my bedroom door. I got up, he has Dad, and we headed out of the apartment and down to my '73

Ford Mustang. It didn't take as long as I had thought to get there. The traffic was surprisingly light.

When we arrived at the cemetery, we stopped at the main office to let them know we were here and to give Dad to them, so they could do what they needed to do. This was all new and weird to me. I'd been here dozens of times with Aunt Hat when she would bring flowers for her parents, who were my grandparents. But I hadn't been to a burial before.

We told them that we would be out at the plot waiting for the couple of people who were going to be there. The Griffins showed up; they were longtime family friends. Then there was Cece, who was one of Aunt Hat's closest friends. And then there was Richard and me. That was it.

For the important man my father used to be, this seemed to be such a minuscule crowd. The service itself was brief, conducted by the head of the cemetery, who was a pastor and said a few words. No one else wanted to speak. As they were about to lower the urn into the ground, I bent over and put a single red rose with Dad and told him I loved him one last time.

Since there were so few of us, it didn't take us long to speak to everyone. They all expressed their condolences and we graciously said thank you. We promised to stay in touch, then went our separate ways. My brother and I left in my car and drove back to my apartment.

Richard would still be staying a few more days, as the Long Beach Grand Prix was that Sunday, March 15th. He just happened to have two tickets because a friend of his couldn't go at the last minute. So, he asked me if I wanted to go. Sure, I'd never been to a real Grand Prix before. Even though I still had to wear this stupid neck brace, that was going to be fun.

But I must admit, it does help; when I go without it, I start to get a headache after a short bit. Sure hope I don't have to wear it much longer.

Sunday was here before I knew it. Richard wanted to leave at six in the morning because we had to drive from the San Fernando Valley down to Long Beach, find a parking place and all that jazz. I couldn't say I was thrilled with the time we were leaving. Once again, I brought my pillow and blanket, crawled into the back of the VW van, laid down, and slept the entire way to Long Beach.

We arrived in town at about 7:30, but it took another half an hour to find a parking place. My brother was a little on the cheap side and wouldn't pay for close parking, not thinking of me in my condition. It hadn't even been three weeks since the accident. I was still in my fashionable, cream-colored neck brace. I felt that I looked stupid, but I knew I needed to wear it or I would regret it.

Before we went to find the section where we belonged, we stopped at the concessions stand to each get a hot dog and something to drink. I was very hungry by this time. I put everything on my hot dog: onions, ketchup, mustard, and pickle relish. It was delicious. I couldn't wait to get to our seats, I had to have a bite. Just as I opened my mouth to chomp down, someone called my name.

"Judy. Judy. Behind you."

I turned around and found myself staring into the face of the devil himself, Michael. I felt the blood drain from my face, which probably went chalk white. I somehow eeked out, "Oh! Hello."

"Hello?" Michael snapped in his usual gruff tone. "That's all you have for me? Who's this you're with?"

"Michael, this is my brother, Richard. Richard, Michael."

"So, what happened to you?" Michael asked. "Why the neck brace?"

"I was in a car accident." I had no intention of going into detail with him. I was shocked enough to see him. It was like that line in *Casablanca* that expresses the bizarre experience of seeing one particular person somewhere that you never expected. Michael just happened to be at the same place as me at the same time. I could hardly contain myself.

"I'm so sorry to hear that," he said. "Are you going to be okay?"

"I'll be just fine, thank you. Well, we need to be getting to our seats."

"It was wonderful running into you, Judy. You take care of yourself now."

I turned and walked off.

Beside me, my brother was looking a little inquisitive, and said, "He seems like a real sleazeball. Where do you know him from?"

"Oh, very intuitive of you," I said with a sharp tone. "I had the pleasure of meeting him through a friend of mine. Trust me, I do not care for the man. I wish we hadn't run into him, and I'm going to do my best to enjoy the rest of the day, anyhow."

We headed off to our seats, where we ate our hot dogs and drank our sodas. It was very loud as the cars whizzed by. They were so fast, it was incredible. The powerful roar of their engines vibrated in my chest. What an exciting afternoon! I had to admit, for not liking me too much, this was really nice of Richard to bring me here with him.

When it was all over, we had to wade our way through the sea of people, all trying to leave at the same time. That was the only downfall to the entire experience. By this time, the pain pill I had taken hours before was no longer working. With all the walking today, my entire body was sore, especially my neck, even with the brace.

When we finally made our way back to his van, I told him I was returning to the back to lay down. I must have fallen asleep not too long after. Before I knew it, we were back at my apartment. It was late and I was so ready for my waterbed. Every part of me hurt. We said our good nights, and I went on into my room to sleep.

The next morning, I heard Richard up at six, so I put my robe on and joined him in the living room. I knew he would want to get an early start to drive straight through to Medford. Little did I know, he had no intention of stopping in Medford on the way home to see Mom. He was driving directly to Albany, about three hours north of Medford.

"Okay," he said, "I've got everything in the van. I'm taking off now."

"Okay. Please drive safe, especially if you're driving the entire way. Please stop and pull over if you get tired."

"Don't worry. I'll be just fine."

I walked him to the front door of the apartment building and waved to him as he drove off. Now, finally, my apartment was my own again. I couldn't wait to get back in there, close the door, and not see or talk with anyone. I so desperately needed to be completely alone.

I wandered around my apartment for a good couple of days. Not answering the phone, not answering the door, with my only visitor being Nora from downstairs. I told her I wanted to be alone for a few days. She totally understood.

That following Saturday, before doing anything, I took out the coke vial and poured some out on the mirror. I wanted to be numb. Maybe if I were numb, none of this would have existed. It would have all been a very bad dream. *Oh, I only wish.*

After I put the mirror back in the bathroom and the vial of coke away, I picked up the unsmoked joint from the ashtray, lighting it. I smoked that one as I rolled another one. I started thinking about Dad and how much I missed him. I spent most of the day like this, numbing myself to not feel the emptiness, the hole in my heart that only my daddy could fill.

I sat on the couch thinking back on the last four months. My, it was so amazing how your life can change in the blink of an eye. One minute you're happily moving through life, and the next thing you know, you're getting slapped in the face with something horrible and totally unexpected. I could walk out of my apartment and get hit by a bus and not come home tonight.

I had too many close calls in the last few months that I truly was surprised that I was not dead. Why had I come so close on a couple of occasions and not die, but Dad did? It wasn't fair. But I did guess that parents are supposed to go before you. One should never lose a child.

I had my knees pulled up to my chest while sitting on the couch, in the spot that Michael always took when he was here. I immediately moved to the other end of the couch.

What an ass. I am really proud of myself for holding it together that day I saw him at the races. I never want to see that man again.

He made me regret ever getting involved with that insurance scam. Why did I listen to Tom? What did it matter now? We didn't even speak to each other anymore. I figured, when you do something wrong, you pay for it in some form or another. My penalty for what I did was losing Tom. He was my first love, and will always have a place in my heart.

It was time to forget all of that. I needed to forget the last nine months and move on with my life. I had a career I wanted to pursue. Life was a never-ending chain of events that, depending on the choices you make, determines the path you will walk. Sometimes it's not the right path, but that you can change. If you feel you're on the wrong path, try another. Life is too short to not live it to the fullest.

24 Hours in Reno

IT HAD BEEN A GOOD WEEK NOW AND MY FRIENDS WERE starting to get worried about me. Raelyn, who was once my roommate, had been calling all week. She was very concerned for me.

The phone rang and it was her:

"Judy, I know you're there. Pick up the phone or I'm coming over, and it won't be pretty."

I picked up the receiver. "Hello, Raelyn, I'm okay. You don't need to worry about me."

"I'm not worried about you, I'm tired of you hiding in your apartment. Life goes on. Look, how about going to a concert tonight? I have a couple of really good tickets."

I shook my head. "I really don't feel like going out."

"I bet you change your mind when you hear," Raelyn said. "I've got two front row seats for Tom Waits and Leon Redbone. Are you interested now?"

"Really? How did you get those?"

Raelyn said, "My friend Ron is Tom Waits' road manager. When I told him I needed to cheer up a dear girlfriend, he gave me the tickets."

"Front row? Really?"

"One night only," she said. "I'll pick you up at five, that way we can get a bite to eat beforehand. I'm sure you haven't been eating, at least not good food. How many bags of Oreos have you gone through?"

She knew me too well. "Yes, I've been a little depressed. But I see a shrink in a couple of days. It would be good for me to get out. I haven't been out to have a good time in months."

"Okay, then. I'll see you at five. Talk to you later."

"Bye, Raelyn."

She picked me up right on time. We went to the Sunset Bar and Grill for dinner. I had a really nice, juicy steak with garlic mashed potatoes. The steak seemed to melt in my mouth. It was delicious! Raelyn got the liver and onions. It reminded me of my mother's liver and onions. We finished up and got to the theater, where they were playing in plenty of time.

We were in the lobby when someone said, "Raelyn, over here."

It was her friend, Ron, who got us the tickets.

Raelyn said, "Hello, Ron. Ron, I'd like you to meet Judy. Judy, this is Ron."

I smiled. "Hello, it's nice to meet you."

"Oh, the pleasure is mine," Ron said. "Raelyn has told me a lot about you. I hope you enjoy the music tonight. And I'm so sorry for your loss."

"Thank you, Ron. I appreciate it. And thank you very much for these tickets. I just love Leon Redbone. Tom is very good, too."

Ron smiled. "Well, you ladies enjoy the show and I will be in touch with you in the next 24 hours."

As Ron walked off, Raelyn and I went to our seats. This was going to be a fabulous show. Leon Redbone played first. I believe I have every record he has put out. I love his old folksy style, and his voice is so deep, it seems to penetrate your soul when he sings.

Tom Waits was up next. I had to admit, I didn't really follow him much. I had listened to his music when Raelyn and I would be working on a project and she put him on the phonograph. His voice was also unique—course and gravelly. I actually enjoyed it once he got through a couple of songs. It was a good night, and Raelyn was a very good friend for getting me out.

I had really needed my friends to drag me out. Lord knows, I wasn't going to come out on my own. After the concert, we went back to my apartment, Raelyn spent the night, as she needed to use my workroom for a project she was working on. I had more room for her to spread out. Plus, I had an overlock machine, which she didn't have.

The next morning, the aroma of coffee was wafting through the air, into my bedroom. I do appreciate the smell of good coffee. I joined Raelyn in the living room—her with coffee, and me with Dr. Pepper. We talked about the night before and how good the concert was.

"Thank you so much for getting me out last night," I said. "I truly appreciate your friendship. It means a lot to me, Raelyn."

She cast a caring look at me. "Why, thank you, Judy. I know you would do the same for me. I don't like seeing my good friends hurting, and you've hurt long enough. Time to get back to the world."

Later that morning, I was cleaning up the apartment a bit, and Raelyn was working in the workroom. I wasn't expecting any visitors, so I was surprised when someone knocked at my door. I looked through the peephole. It was Ron from the night before; I let him in.

"Well, what a surprise," I said. "How are you doing this morning?"

"I'm great!" Ron said. "How about yourself? Is Raelyn here? She said she would be here working today."

"Hey, Raelyn! Ron is here. Come on out!" I shouted from the living room.

"Have a seat, Ron."

"Oh, no thanks, I'm good."

Raelyn emerged from the workroom.

"Well, good morning, Ron. What's up?"

Ron looked excited. "How would you two girls like to go to Vegas for the day? Coke's on me."

"Wow," Raelyn said. "That sounds great, but I have a project I have to finish in just a couple of days. There's no way I can go, I'm sorry. Judy, how about you?"

"Wow, I don't know," I said. "It sounds like fun."

"Do you like to gamble, Judy? And if so, what do you play?"

"I love to play Blackjack."

Ron answered, "Then, you drive. I've got the coke, so let's go have fun for 24 hours!"

"Sounds good to me," I said. "I do need to get out of the slump I've been in. Let me throw a couple things in a bag and I'm ready."

I went into my bedroom, got into my hiding place in my nightstand to get out a couple hundred dollars for gambling.

Then, I threw a couple of things in a bag, and I was ready for this little adventure.

"All righty. I'm all set."

Raelyn walked us to the door and wished us well. We had a great trip until we hit the mountains going over to Las Vegas. It was starting to snow.

"I don't know about this, Ron. If it keeps snowing, I'm going to have to turn around. I don't know if Raelyn told you or not, but just before my father died, I was run over by a semi-truck in a snow storm going over the Siskiyou Pass. I'm a little concerned."

Before I could make up my mind to definitely turn around, my mind was made up for me. The California Highway Patrol officers were stopping the cars heading east over the pass because of a snowstorm. I was more than happy to turn around. However, a little disappointed that we weren't going to have a good time gambling. Then, Ron had a suggestion.

"Judy, how about instead of going back to your place, let's go to LAX and see if we can get a round trip to Reno for the night?"

"Hm, that sounds interesting. I really do like gambling in Reno better than Vegas," I said. "It's not as expensive and easier to get to a different casino if you want. Sure! That sounds like a plan to me."

We headed for LAX. I found the two-day parking area and got us a good spot. Into the terminal we went. I didn't even bother with the bag I packed, I only took my purse. I don't remember what airline we flew, but we got a flight out within the hour, and a return flight the next morning at eleven. We booked it. Ron was gracious enough to pick up the tab for the two tickets.

"Thank you, Ron. That's very nice of you."

"Hey, the pleasure is all mine. I'm just glad you were up for the adventure. I enjoy doing things in the spur of the moment."

Next thing I knew, we were on the plane having drinks, and before we could get a second round, we were descending into the Reno airport. We hopped a cab and went straight to Harrah's. It was my favorite place in Reno. On my 21st birthday, my mother and Aunt Hat had brought me to Reno and we stayed at Harrah's. One of the best birthdays of my life.

Ron had a little bullet. It was an attachment that you screwed onto a vial of coke. You turn the lever one way and it fills the little compartment with a hit of coke, then you turn the lever back, hold it up to your nostril, and take a hit. Quite ingenious and very convenient. He passed it to me and told me to head into the ladies' room and help myself. Fortunately, I did have to pee, as well. I went into the stall, locking the door behind me. I stood there, flushed the toilet, and took a couple of hits. After I finished, I rejoined Ron on the floor of the casino.

"I spotted the Blackjack tables," he said. "Shall we?"

He bowed and gestured with his right arm towards the tables, allowing me to go first. We found a great table that had two spots open, and one was what they call "Third Base." It was the last seat at the table. I preferred that spot because you could see all the cards that were played before it was your turn.

It was the perfect seat if you were counting cards. But I'm not a card counter. I've tried, but it's too much work. I like to enjoy myself and not worry about anything except whether the dealer has a Blackjack or not. Most card counters like to play with a single, or at most, a double deck shoe. I personally like the eight-deck shoe. It's almost impossible to count cards, so why try? It allows me the freedom to not worry if the deck is loaded with face cards or not.

We were ordering drinks as we played and taking bathroom breaks for more hits of coke. We both went up and down with our chips, then they switched dealers on us, and both of us started winning. This was a couple hours in. We were having a blast. Then, the cards turned on us. I recognized it right away and knew it was time to take our winnings and move on.

"Hey, Ron, you're up several hundred dollars, aren't you?"

"Yeah, I am."

"Let's take a walk." We both cashed in our chips for larger ones and left that table.

"What's up, Judy? We were winning."

"Yes, we were, before they switched dealers on us again. Then didn't you notice that we both lost five hands in a row? Time to move on to a fresh table."

"Boy, Judy. You sound like you've done this before."

"I dated a card shark for a bit and he taught me a few things. Let's go next door to the Nevada Club. It's a great place to play Blackjack."

The Nevada Club was this little hole-in-the-wall place situated between Harrah's and Harold's Club, two rather popular casinos in their day. When you walked in, you got a distinct aroma of booze and vintage. It wasn't a bad smell. It created an atmosphere compared to the larger, newer casinos. On the first floor was the bar that stretched the length of the club. In front of the bar were the many Blackjack tables, all with varying limits. I personally liked the two-dollar tables, but since Ron and I were both up, we found a five-dollar limit table and sat there.

It seemed louder in there than the larger casinos. The bells of the slot machines were going off right and left. People were standing all around the craps table as someone had a hot streak going. Everyone was yelling and carrying on. It all added to the atmosphere of the place. It was like being in an old saloon in a western.

Hours flew by in the Nevada Club. We had been winning, drinking, and doing blow in the bathrooms; it was a ton of fun. The sort of good time I needed to help get over the shock of my dad being gone. Besides the concert Raelyn and I went to, this was the most fun I had in the last year. I was well overdue. Soon, the sun was rising, and night was turning to dawn, and dawn into day.

"Judy, how about we cash in and go find some breakfast?"

"Sure," I said. "The Cal-Neva has a great, cheap breakfast. Let's go over there."

When we finished eating, we still had a couple hours before our plane back to LA, so we sat down at the Blackjack tables at the Cal-Neva. We both did pretty good there, too. After an hour, we were both up again and decided to go ahead and call it. We took our chips to the cashier. Surprisingly, I was up about $300, and Ron had won about $700. He was betting heavier than I was.

We caught a cab and headed back to the airport in Reno to catch our flight home. What a whirlwind trip that was, and just what the doctor had ordered, minus the cocaine, for sure. We landed at LAX at about one, and headed into Hollywood. Our light breakfast made us both starving by now, and Ron suggested that we go to the Sunset Grill (made famous in a Don Henley song).

When we arrived, we walked in to find Tom Waits having his breakfast at about 2:30 in the afternoon. Ron went up to say hello and he invited us to join him. The two talked business while I took in the scenery. It was a bright day in LA, but inside the grill, it was dark and quiet, with only one other couple in there besides us. I was facing the window and enjoyed watching the people walking up and down Sunset Boulevard.

There was quite the variety; a couple of hookers walked past in their short-shorts and platform heels, donning some interesting wigs.

Then you had your good-looking men walking by, but not to worry, they certainly were not interested in looking my way. They were strolling for an afternoon good time. Lastly, you had your tourists, who stuck out like sore thumbs. Not too many of them, as they usually didn't make it that far west down Sunset Blvd; they tended to stay closer to Grauman's Chinese Theatre on Hollywood Boulevard, which ran parallel to Sunset.

When we finished with breakfast, we headed back to my apartment, where Raelyn was still working.

"Hello, Raelyn, are you still here?" I yelled as we walked into the living room.

She emerged from the workroom looking like she had been up all night, which she had. Ron left her some coke since she couldn't join us. She had gotten quite a bit accomplished overnight; I was very surprised. She had a men's tie business; she made hand-painted silk ties that were absolutely stunning. Raelyn managed to make several dozen ties and had her order almost filled.

We visited for a very brief time as everyone was tired. But I couldn't help saying to Raelyn, "You really missed a great time. We ended up flying to Reno for the night and played Blackjack the whole trip. We even won. But the best part was, when we got home, we went to the Sunset Grill for breakfast, and Tom Waits was in there. I had breakfast with Tom Waits."

"Are you kidding me?" Raelyn exclaimed. "Crap!!! I would have died to have eaten breakfast with him. Damn, you lucked out. I'm jealous!!!"

"Well, girls," Ron said. "You two talk, and tell her all about it, Judy. I'm going home to crash. I had a great adventure with you, Judy. Thanks for going."

"Oh, no. Thank you. I had a blast. It was just what I needed."

I walked him to the door, showing him out.

"Thanks again," I said. "Drive safe."

I closed the door and went back in the apartment.

"Well, I don't know about you, Raelyn, but I'm going to bed. I'm wiped out."

Raelyn nodded. "I'm going to finish up here and head on back to my place. I need to get some sleep myself. You sleep well, and I'll talk to you later. Thanks for letting me use your workroom, it helped getting all those ties done at once. See you later."

"Lock the door on your way out, would you, please? Bye."

Into bed I crawled and slept from about five that afternoon until eight o'clock the next morning. I was beat, but that was what you get for partying a little too much.

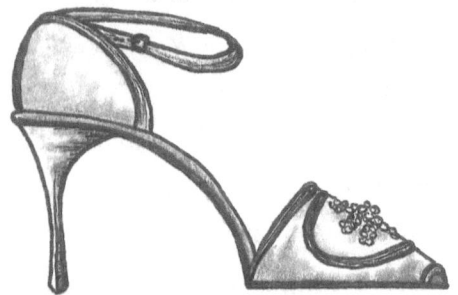

Shoe Shopping

A COUPLE OF DAYS WENT BY AND MY GIRLFRIEND PAMELA hadn't heard from me in about a week. She, too, had been concerned about my state of mind after experiencing everything I had gone through in the last few months. She decided that it was time that I started getting out more, so she gave me a call.

"Hey, Judy, you need to get out. Come on over to my place, I've found this fabulous new discount designer shoe store in Hollywood. It's spectacular; you'll love it!"

"That sounds interesting," I said. "I just happen to have an extra $300 laying around. I'll tell you all about it when I see you."

"Great. When can you be here?"

"Well, it's 10:30. I can be there by noon. Does that work for you?"

"Yeah, that's perfect," Pamela said. "It will take me that long to get ready."

"All righty, I'll see you then. Bye." I hung up and jumped in the shower. After I was ready, I got in my car and headed over the hill into Hollywood. It was easiest to take surface streets to Pamela's place. I went straight up Laurel Canyon, past the Canyon Market at the top of the hill. My dry cleaners was situated right behind the market. Then, down into Hollywood from there.

I arrived at Pamela's place, parked, and went up to her apartment. She was finishing up. Her apartment was one big closet. I thought I had clothes, but she had tons. Mostly vintage outfits. The fact that she was almost six feet tall, she looked stunning in just about everything.

"So," I said, "tell me about this shoe place. How did you find it?"

"My girlfriend, Bonnie, and I were walking along Hollywood Boulevard and came across it. It's fabulous. You'll love it. Let's go."

We took my car and drove to the shoe store, found a parking place in back, and went on in. It was full of shoe racks everywhere you turned. The customers were abundant. Apparently, the lesser expensive shoes were on the first floor, and the Italian designer heels were upstairs. I followed Pamela as she headed straight for the stairs and up she went. I adore Pamela; I look up to her as the big sister I never had. She is a couple years older than me, and wise beyond her years.

Pamela and I had met when I was doing a fashion show for the Hollywood Palladium. I had made my "Butterfly" dress to the specific measurements for a model who ended up dropping out on me at the last minute. So, the Palladium hired a model to fit the measurements of my dress, and the model they hired was Pamela. I was very guarded of my dress design. I was being very careful as to who could see it.

We were both sitting in the reception area of the fashion show coordinator's office when I was called in. They explained that they had found another model for me, and she had the correct measurements but was a pinch taller, which was totally fine by me. They then called Pamela into the office and introduced us to each other.

All of a sudden, it was like I was meeting someone I knew before, possibly from another lifetime. We connected instantly; she was perfect, not only as my model, but as my dear friend whom I totally admire. She's that true, strong, independent, take-no-shit kind of gal. She taught me a lot about the streets and the ways of telling bullshitters. If I haven't said it before, I'm saying it now: I absolutely admire and adore this woman.

Needless to say, we became fast friends and the interesting thing was that my first apartment in LA in the Miracle Mile District was just two blocks over from Pamela's street. We had lived near one another for a year before we met. When we did finally meet, I had moved out to the valley, the San Fernando Valley in Studio City, right at the base of the Hollywood Hills.

So, getting back to shoe shopping. When I reached the top floor and saw all the racks of shoes, I was in heaven. I immediately found my size section and started browsing through all the beautiful high heels that were lined up like the Radio City Rockettes. Dozens upon dozens of shoes priced everywhere from $65 to $350 or $400 tops. These shoes were already reduced at least 50%, if not 75%, from their retail prices. I didn't know where the store owners were from, or what were their connections to get all these fabulous shoes, but I tell you, it was spectacular.

I picked out a couple pairs that I couldn't live without. One pair was navy blue suede with red leather piping all around the edges. They had a good four-inch heel, with the cutest red seed bead flower at the toe. The other pair would go perfect with a dress I had recently designed; they were black and white leather strips woven in and out to form a checkerboard pattern. They had an open toe and fit like a dream. There is nothing like the fit of a good shoe. I remember a pair of Kate Spades high heel sandals I owned. I could wear those shoes all day and they would still be comfortable.

Walking out of the store to my car, we were talking about the buys we got and how wonderful that store was. It became my new favorite place to shop. I took Pamela on home and headed back over the hill to my place.

When I got home, I put my new shoes on the couch and retrieved the mirror and the vial of coke. I laid everything out on the coffee table and dumped what little coke I had left in the vial onto the mirror. I sat back on the couch, lighting a joint, staring at the little pile of white powder. Looking at the bag with my two pair of shoes in it, I opened one of the boxes, taking out the navy pair and setting one on the table. I then opened up the other box, retrieving one of the shoes and placing that shoe on the table.

I sat back again, smoking my joint, looking back and forth from the coke to the shoes. Being into fashion as I was, I let the sensible side of me speak. Now, for $300, I realized the two choices that were so obvious: I could go visit Joe Blow. Now, don't laugh, his nickname was really Joe Blow, as he was the main supplier of coke to all the famous singer/song writers who lived in Laurel Canyon. Don't quote me, but a certain Joni Mitchell song always made me wonder if it was about the women there.

The other choice I had was, $300 later, I had two fabulous pair of sexy high heels. Of these two choices, which one would I give up, because I certainly could not afford both of these habits. Well, that was the beginning of the end of my coke-buying days. In fact, after this realization, I didn't buy coke again, but I certainly would not turn it down if it was offered. No, I would much rather have something tangible that would last and be used over and over. The choice was very clear: *I'll take the shoes! Thank you very much.*

After that mindshift, I chopped up the last of the coke, divided it into two small lines, snorted both, and gave them a grand send off. It wasn't like I would miss it. The only thing really worthwhile about it was that you can accomplish a lot when consuming coke. Now, I'm not advocating coke at all, I'm just saying that back in the day, yes, I did party on it occasionally, but I felt it was best used for getting things done. That's all.

I figured if that was the last of the coke, *let's accomplish something.* I put the shoes back in their rightful boxes and took them into my bedroom. My closet was the length of the west wall. I slid open the folding doors and organized my shoe assortment. I got out my masking tape and a Sharpie. I liked to keep my shoes in their original boxes whenever possible, so I put the tape on the box and wrote a brief description of the shoes inside. Made it easier to find what I was looking for.

Then I returned to the living room, sitting down on my side of the couch, and rolled another joint. I sipped my Dr. Pepper that was on the table, picked up the ashtray and lighter, and lit the joint. I relaxed into the comfort of my couch and thought of everything that had happened to me in the last six months.

I have only God and Angel Bob to thank for my still being on this earth. I am also thankful for a very good reason to justify why I should no longer buy coke. Yes, I admit I enjoy the drug, but to me, a working-class citizen, I work too hard for what I earn, and dang it, I am going to have something to show for it besides a deviated septum.

The Quaalude Poster

SINCE I AM TALKING ABOUT PAMELA, I SHOULD SHARE THIS story with you. You should enjoy it. Pamela called me up one morning to ask me what I was doing that afternoon and evening. I had nothing planned, so she invited me to go on a modeling shoot with her. She didn't say what it was for and said we could go out for drinks when she was done. I believe it was a Friday night, so it sounded like something that would be fun.

I enjoyed watching Pamela work, whether she was modeling or singing. I loved going into the studio with her when she was recording. There was always a wide variety of people at the recording sessions. It was a good way of networking and partying at the same time. I had to admit, I did enjoy hanging out with musicians; they were a fun group and Pamela knew a wide assortment. I met musicians, the likes of Aaron Neville to Joe Walsh, Dan Fogelberg, Stevie Wonder—we went to one of Stevie's birthday parties!—and a lot of unknowns in between. It was great fun.

If you have ever seen the documentary called *Echo in the Canyon* by Jakob Dylan (Bob Dylan's son), it lays out what the music scene was like in Laurel Canyon back in the day. It's an excellent documentary if you haven't seen it. I highly recommend it.

Anyway, getting back to this modeling gig Pamela had. I went to pick her up at her place and we went to a studio in Hollywood. She was to get naked and lay amongst a shit-load of lemons. They had cases of fresh-picked lemons. It was then that I found out the shoot was for Lemon Quaaludes. However, it wasn't for another hour that I learned the real reason that Pamela invited me along. She finished a session, put on her bathrobe, and we went into her dressing room.

"How's the champagne treating you?" she asked.

"Oh, it's quite good. I just have to be careful not to drink too much."

"We're all here to have a good time as well as create art," she said. "So, Judy, do you think you'd like to join in?"

"What?" I was shocked. "What did you just say?"

"I was wondering if you would like to be the other model?"

"What do you mean, 'other model?'"

"Well, I have to admit," Pamela said. "I did have an ulterior motive for inviting you tonight. Now, don't get upset or mad; you don't have to do anything you don't want to. They need two girls, and the second girl is a no-show. Would you like to take her place?" Pamela was being very serious.

"Would I have to get naked, too?"

"Yes," she said, "but the only thing that will be showing on you is your backside."

"In other words, my ass?"

Pamela went on to explain, "Look, the whole premise is to have me laying on my back with my front side up and exposed, while you lay upside down from me on your stomach, so only your backside is showing. No one will ever see your face. Once we're in that position, they will pile the lemons on us and all around us. We'll basically be buried in lemons. So, you see, you really don't need to worry about anyone recognizing you."

Pamela paused as she could see I was actually contemplating it.

"Besides, who else will be able to say, 'That's my fine ass on that Quaalude poster?'" She gave me that look, like it was all going to be all right, and continued,

"You do know you have a very nice ass with spectacular legs, Judy! You really should take this opportunity to show off what you do have. Come on, plus I'll split the $500 with you. Sound good now? That's another pair or two of high heels."

I handed her my glass and said, "Please go fill this up for me and make sure there's a robe I can put on, 'cause I'm not walking out there in front of everyone naked. If I'm going to do it, I'll have the robe on until I lay down. Okay?"

"Okay. One more champagne, coming up." Pamela left the dressing room and I was thinking, *the only way I can do this is if I have a slight buzz.*

When she came back with my liquid courage, she also had a small vial of coke with a coke spoon that one of the photographers had given her in case I needed a little extra persuading. I took a couple of hits from the vial, as did Pamela. I proceeded to undress all the way down to nothing, taking the robe from her. It was your generic white terry cloth robe you would find at any spa or hotel.

I chased the hits of coke with a drink of champagne, took a good look at Pamela and said,

"Okay, let's do this. But first, give me another couple of hits and let me finish the champagne."

I was finally relieved of some of my inhibitions about being naked in front of people. I figured this was their job; they saw naked people all the time, and I was certainly nothing special. We walked over to the mat on the white backdrop. Pamela directed me as to what to do.

"Okay, Judy, lay down on your stomach and stretch out with your arms above your head. I'm going to lay next to you with my feet at your head and vice versa, only on my back. Our waist and hips will naturally curve into one another. Once I do that, they will cover us with the lemons. Piece of cake."

I knelt on my knees, removing my robe and handing it to Pamela as I lay down completely with my arms stretched upwards. She lay next to me, our skin touching. I was so glad this was Pamela, because there is no way I would have done it with anyone else. I did feel myself relaxing after a few moments of lying there, while the photographer moved around us in a circle, taking shots from up above us. This went on for almost an hour, even though it didn't feel like it had taken that long.

When they were done with all the shots they were going to take, Pamela and I were able to get up, putting on our robes to go get dressed again.

I must say, I still had a nice little buzz going and actually remember telling Pamela, "I have to admit, that was kind of fun once I didn't care about people looking at me. And it's going to be interesting seeing my butt on a Quaalude poster without anyone being able to tell it's me. BUT... Don't you dare do this to me again!!! Do you understand? No hijacking me for naked shoots. Tell me beforehand, so I know what I'm walking into. Not that I'm ready to do this again, mind you. All I can say is, that it was interesting."

Pamela and I hung out for a bit, then we collected our cash and excused ourselves from the party. I must say, that wasn't a bad way to make $250. But I believe that was my modeling career, there would be no more. We got in my car and drove off.

"Pamela, do you still want to go out for drinks? It's getting a little on the late side."

"Yeah, that took longer than I thought it would. No, let's call it a night. I need to get a good night's sleep, because I'm singing tomorrow night in the valley at that little jazz club. You are coming, aren't you?"

"You bet, I am," I said. "I wouldn't miss it. Yes, bed sounds real good to me right about now. Thanks for sharing the modeling fee."

"Heck, you deserved it," Pamela said. "You earned it, and you did a great job. I'm very proud of you."

I pulled up to her apartment building. Pamela hopped out and said she'll talk to me tomorrow. We said our good nights and I drove off into the darkened LA night.

My Overdose

I DON'T KNOW IF YOU WOULD CALL THIS A BRUSH WITH DEATH or not, but I did start my drug-taking at an early age, and I started it with an overdose. I don't remember my exact age, but it was either four or five—very young.

I wasn't interested in the "drug" part of the equation; I liked the taste. It was orange-flavored baby aspirin. Those little orange pills were bursting with sweet orange flavor. They were so delicious that I remember wanting to share them with one of the neighbor kids.

I remember having Debbie in my parents' back bathroom with me. I told her there was some special candy that my mother kept and only gave it to me when I was sick. I remember really talking up this baby aspirin, how delicious it was, and how she had to try some with me. I don't know exactly how many we each ate, but it was enough to get us a trip to the hospital to have our stomachs pumped. That is one thing I do remember very clearly. But I'm getting ahead of myself.

I don't know how it got back to our mothers that we had eaten the baby aspirin. I know I didn't tell. I do remember after we were found out, the grownups were talking about taking us to the hospital. I was on the front porch of the house asking my big brother to hide me so I didn't have to go, but he wouldn't.

I know they took us in the family car, and the next thing I remember was being taken into a room that was big and white. There were nurses and a doctor all dressed in white with masks on. It was quite frightening to a child my age, and very overwhelming. My parents were not in the room with me, just these strangers.

They put me up on the gurney, then had me lay down and turn on my right side. Next, they came at me with this long, black rubber hose-looking device, had me open my mouth, and they stuck it down my throat as far as it would go. I immediately started vomiting into a bucket they held under my chin. For a child who was four or five years old, this was extremely traumatic.

I don't remember what, if anything, happened after that, other than going home. Trust me when I say I wouldn't go near a pill for a very long time after that. No, thank you.

The Train Accident

I HAVE NO EXCUSE FOR THE TRAIN ACCIDENT OTHER THAN I was young and stupid at the ripe age of seventeen. I was two hundred miles from home this particular weekend with my sister-in-law and my baby nephew. She lived in a very small town in Oregon called Lebanon. My brother was stationed in Germany at the time—the Viet Nam era. I was there visiting with a girlfriend named Kayla; she lived another small town away called Sweet Home.

My sister-in-law had a small, one-bedroom apartment that was upstairs, above a garage. I remember the wood stairs going up the side of the garage to her front door; the paint was old and flaking off. The whole place could have used a new paint job, house included. Kayla had come over to visit to see her boyfriend that night. She and I took off in her car to meet up with the boyfriend and his friend.

We met them at the local hamburger spot, where I was introduced to the friend, Mike. Kayla and her boyfriend took off in

her car and we were left with Mike's Mustang. They said they would be back in an hour, but didn't say where they were going. We talked about nothing in particular, ate a hamburger, and had a chocolate shake. An hour came and went, and we were getting anxious.

Mike suggested that we go look for them, and I agreed. We drove to the usual spots where kids hung out and couldn't find them anywhere. Driving on the outskirts of town, we came to a little knoll in the road with railroad tracks running down it and stopped there. We were discussing where to look for them next.

I was leaning up against the passenger's door facing Mike as he was talking. I had grown up in the country near railroad tracks, so I knew a little about them. As I was sitting there listening to Mike talk, I found myself looking past him and down the tracks we were on. About a hundred yards down was a light for the trains. It is usually red, but this time it was most definitely green. I sat there puzzled for a moment. That light was only supposed to be green when a train was coming.

I turn to my right in the seat, looking down the tracks. All I see is a huge, round, white headlight of a locomotive about fifty feet from us. I manage to squeak out: "TRAIN!"

Mike threw the gearshift knob into reverse and backed his green Mustang off the tracks, enough that the engine of the train did not hit me square in the door where it was headed. It caught the front fender and dragged us along the tracks for a bit, until we finally bounced off the train and away from the tracks. The train came to a full stop about the same time we did. Several people got out to assess the damage and to see if we were all right.

From that point, I must have been in shock because I don't remember how we got back to my sister-in-law's apartment.

The next thing I remember is sitting on the living room floor at my sister-in-law's. I was playing with the baby. All of a sudden, out of nowhere, I doubled over in the most excruciating pain in my right rib area. I could hardly breathe. I could breathe, it just hurt like hell every time I did. We discussed taking me to the emergency room, but I was not interested in going. My parents would find out and that was the last thing I wanted. They would have grounded me until I was thirty.

I went back home to my parents in Medford and never did say a word about it. I stayed in my room and figured the pain would pass, and it did, but very slowly. I was determined not to let my parents know anything was wrong.

It wasn't until about eighteen years later that I was starting to experience chest pains in my right ribs. I was married at the time, living in Oregon and under tremendous amount of stress. The pain went on for quite some time before I said I was going to see my doctor in Los Angeles for a complete physical.

It wasn't until I saw him that I found out what my issue was. He took a chest x-ray as part of the physical. I remember him walking back into the exam room and asking me, "So, when did you break your four ribs?"

I was stunned. I had to sit and think about what could have possibly happened to cause this? It took a few moments, but then it came to me: "The only thing I can think of is when I got hit by a train."

"Excuse me, you were hit by a train?" the doctor asked.

"Yes, when I was seventeen and not where I was supposed to be. It must have been when I was slammed into the passenger door and hit the arm rest. That's the only thing I can think of that would have caused this."

The doctor explained, "Well, Judy, getting hit by a train would most certainly qualify for the reason behind your four broken ribs that did not heal properly. Because of that, you now have arthritis in your ribs. The bad news is that there is nothing we can do about them now."

"So, this is a pain that I'm going to have to learn to live with?"

"That's correct."

It turns out that I cannot comfortably sleep on my right side on a regular mattress. If I do, I wake up with my right side hurting so much that it's difficult to breathe. This is why, for the last forty-one years, I still sleep on a waterbed.

Epilogue

THE ONE VERY IMPORTANT MESSAGE I WOULD LIKE YOU to get from this is… Dream! Dream as big as you can. The universe is never ending, so **dare to dream that big!**

The one thing in life you should always strive for is to do something you love. When you're choosing a career path, pick something you're passionate about. If you can make a living at something you love to do, it will never feel like work, and it will be a joy to treasure every day of your life. Life is too short to go to a job every day that you hate. It isn't worth your time. God wants to see you happy, so make sure you do what makes you happy.

But BEWARE!!! There are people, companies, and corporations that don't care about you. All they care about is their bottom line. These are the places you must be careful of.

Take myself as an example. I retired once from my dream job, then found myself bored and went looking for something casual, such as trimming marijuana plants. I was only interested in working several months out of the year. I took this one job with a cannabis company here in Southern Oregon, thinking it would only be part time. When it was looking like they wanted me permanently, I decided that this was a decent job. I liked it, I liked the company, and I loved the people, but then it went corporate.

It so happens that I was writing this book as I was still working for them. I had worked for this company for almost three years and hoped to retire for good from there, which they so kindly helped me with last week. After my hard work, dedication, and loyalty, they laid me off. They totally caught me off guard. The company is going down anyway, so it was only a matter of time. I didn't realize that my time was up now.

I must admit, this was a little stumbling block, which set me off into a slight depression. I couldn't write anything of value for almost a week. I honestly thought they had done me a favor, but for whatever reason, I was grieving the loss of my job.

I must say, though, that my job was no longer my job. I was an office assistant; I did paperwork. Then, last harvest, I was pulled away to buck and trim weed. The next thing I know, they are sending me to the greenhouses to work with the clones, which are cuttings of the marijuana plant that you put into a grow machine where they're sprayed with water and nutrients to sprout roots. Then they're planted in three-by-three-inch pots, where they grow large enough to plant in the earth.

That soon turned into working in the field, which at this point in my life, I have absolutely no desire to be working in the field as a "farm tech." That was their fancy way of saying farmhand.

On one hand, I see myself as bitter and a little insulted that they laid me off. On the other hand, they did me a huge favor. This is another good example of something seeming rotten at the time, but there is a good reason for this happening. With a little time and a good friend to talk to, after about a week, I came out of that slump.

I don't know if you're aware of "angel numbers?" Look up Doreen Virtue and her angel numbers. These are groups of the same three numbers that appear to you at once. Like when you look at the clock and it's 3:33. That group of 3's means something. Learn more by Googling Doreen Virtue, who has written extensively about angel numbers.

For weeks, I was noticing groups of numbers, and as I read the meanings, everything seemed to point at my book being completed and published. One particular angel number conveyed the message that a major life change was coming. It wasn't bad or good, just the nature of reality that the only constant in life is change, and that I should flow gracefully with it. I received this as affirmation that a change with my work situation was imminent.

Around that time, I was telling my Book Coach, Elizabeth Ann Atkins, that after the book was published, I wanted to go on cruises to do book signings. A few weeks later, she came across a comedian who was doing cruises. He told her they were looking for speakers and authors, and directed her to which cruise lines, as well as how to apply. She couldn't wait to tell me about this serendipitous experience that affirmed that the Universe was hearing me and answering my prayers.

I had been manifesting for months, and this was a clear affirmation that I do have a direction to go in now, and it's something I enjoy. You must watch your thoughts, because the Universe is listening. You can manifest something spectacular in your life, or you could draw something unpleasant to you. You must mind your thoughts.

One other reason for me to write this book is expressed in an Elton John song, where he talks about crossing a bridge or fading away. This book series is my bridge. Yes, I want to cross it; no, I don't want to fade away.

Nor should you.

Remember, think big, dream on, and make it happen.

About the Author

JUDY BOHNING IS HAPPILY RETIRED LIVING IN SOUTHERN Oregon where she has had an opportunity to reflect on her roller coaster life.

She spent the majority of her career in the entertainment industry in Hollywood, California in costume and design. She was blessed to start her career with Bette Davis and ended with Betty White, two of the greatest Bettys in the industry.

From her childhood to her retirement, her roller coaster cart has come close numerous times to careening off the tracks, but she just cinched the belt tighter and hung on. Trains, automobiles, trucks, fires, oh, my, somehow kept her creative juices flowing.

Read this book, then ask yourself, *Could* I *have handled the challenges that she faced?*

Judy with Betty White

Stay in Touch with the Author!

Please follow Judy Bohning on her Facebook page to learn about her book signings, media appearances and other exciting news about *Memoirs of an Eccentric Angel*.

https://www.facebook.com/MemoirsOfAnEccentricAngel

You can also contact her via email at
eccentricangel@yahoo.com.

Watch for the next book in her Fire and Ice series in 2023!

End Notes

[1] Thomas A. Edison Quotes. BrainyQuotes.com, BrainyMedia Inc, 2022. https://www.brainyquote.com/quotes/thomas_a_edison_109004

[2] B. C. Forbes Quotes. BrainyQuote.com, BrainyMedia Inc, 2022. https://www.brainyquote.com/quotes/b_c_forbes_126457

www.ingramcontent.com/pod-product-compliance
Lightning Source LLC
Chambersburg PA
CBHW021632120626
46545CB00002B/509